Modern Critical Interpretations

Herman Melville's
Billy Budd, "Benito Cereno,"
"Bartleby the Scrivener,"
and Other Tales

Modern Critical Interpretations

These and other titles in preparation

Herman Melville's
Billy Budd, "Benito Cereno," "Bartleby the Scrivener," and Other Tales

Edited and with an introduction by
Harold Bloom
Sterling Professor of the Humanities
Yale University

Chelsea House Publishers ◊ *1987*
NEW YORK ◊ NEW HAVEN ◊ PHILADELPHIA

Library of Congress Cataloging-in-Publication Data
Herman Melville's Billy Budd, Benito Cereno, Bartleby the
scrivener, and other tales
    (Modern critical interpretations)
    Bibliography: p.
    Includes index.
    Summary: A collection of seven criticial essays on Melville's
shorter works of fiction including "Billy Budd" and "The Piazza
Tales."
    1. Melville, Herman, 1819–1891.—Criticism and
interpretation.   [1. Melville, Herman, 1819–1891.—Criticism
and interpretation. 2. American literature—History and
criticism]   I. Bloom, Harold.   II. Series.
PS2387.H44 1987 813'.3 86–29960
ISBN 1-55546-009-7 (alk. paper)

Contents

Editor's Note

This volume gathers together what I judge to be the best criticism available of Herman Melville's shorter fiction, with a particular emphasis upon *Billy Budd* and *The Piazza Tales*. The essays are arranged here in the chronological order of their original publication. I am grateful to Kevin Pask for his aid in research for this book.

My introduction centers upon "The Bell-Tower," which I believe to be the most undervalued of *The Piazza Tales*. The chronological sequence begins with the late Jorge Luis Borges's prologue to his own translation of "Bartleby the Scrivener." Leo Marx follows with his own parabolic reading of "Bartleby," in which the tale's true subject emerges as Melville himself, a writer who gives up conventional modes in order to immerse himself in the destructive element.

Two very different readings of *Billy Budd* follow. Warner Berthoff finds in the short novel a "compassionate objectivity," a mode in which Melville has ceased to quarrel with God, nature, or society. Working in the deconstructive tradition of Paul de Man, Barbara Johnson locates a "difference" running through *Billy Budd* that "prevents us from ever knowing whether what we hit coincides with what we understand."

"Benito Cereno," the darkest of Melville's tales, is analyzed by Eric J. Sundquist as being finally a reader's choice "between Delano and Cereno," who however are then seen as "nearly tautological possibilities." "Bartleby" returns in a Marxist reading by Michael Paul Rogin, who also examines the grim "The Paradise of Bachelors and the Tartarus of Maids" as another supposed "sketch of working-class life."

In this book's final essay, Michael Clark also turns to "Bartleby," in conjunction with *The Confidence-Man*, and Cotton Mather's *The Wonders of the Invisible World*, in order to trace Melville's nostalgia for interpretive links between language and the world, a nostalgia never to be assayed, unless indeed we find it, as I would, in the great "Whiteness of the Whale" chapter in *Moby-Dick*.

Introduction

I

Melville's *The Piazza Tales* was published in 1856, five years after *Moby-Dick*. Two of the six tales—"Bartleby the Scrivener" and "Benito Cereno"—are commonly and rightly accepted among Melville's strongest works, together with *Moby-Dick* and (rather more tenuously) *The Confidence-Man* and *Billy Budd, Sailor*. Two others—"The Encantadas, or Enchanted Isles" and "The Bell-Tower"—seem to me even better, being equal to the best moments in *Moby-Dick*. Two of the *Piazza Tales* are relative trifles: "The Piazza" and "The Lightning-Rod Man." A volume of novellas with four near-masterpieces is an extraordinary achievement, but particularly poignant if, like Melville, you had lost your reading public after the early success of *Typee* and *Omoo*, the more equivocal reception of *Mardi*, and the return to a wider audience with *Redburn* and even more with *White-Jacket*. *Moby-Dick* today is, together with *Leaves of Grass* and *Huckleberry Finn*, one of the three candidates for our national epic, but like *Leaves of Grass* it found at first only the one great reader (Hawthorne for Melville, Emerson for Whitman) and almost no popular response. What was left of Melville's early audience was killed off by the dreadful *Pierre*, a year after *Moby-Dick*, and despite various modern salvage attempts *Pierre* certainly is unreadable, in the old-fashioned sense of that now critically abused word. You just cannot get through it, unless you badly want and need to do so.

The best of *The Piazza Tales* show the post-*Pierre* Melville writing for himself, possibly Hawthorne, and a few strangers. Himself the sole support of wife, four children, mother, and several sisters, Melville was generally in debt from at least 1855 on, and Hawthorne and Richard Henry Dana, though they tried, could not get the author of *Pierre* appointed to a consulate. In the late 1850s, the tormented and shy Melville

1

attempted the lecture circuit, but as he was neither a pulpit-pounder like Henry Ward Beecher, nor a preternaturally eloquent sage like Ralph Waldo Emerson, he failed rather badly. Unhappily married, mother-ridden, an apparent literary failure; the author of *The Piazza Tales* writes out of the depths. Steeped, as were Carlyle and Ruskin, in the King James Bible, Melville no more believed in the Bible than did Carlyle and Ruskin. But even as *Moby-Dick* found its legitimate and overwhelming precursors in the Bible, Spenser, Shakespeare, and Milton, so do *The Piazza Tales*. Melville's rejection of biblical theology, his almost Gnostic distrust of nature and history alike, finds powerful expression in *The Piazza Tales*, as it did throughout all his later fictional prose and his verse.

II

"The Bell-Tower" is a tale of only fifteen pages but it has such resonance and strength that each rereading gives me the sense that I have experienced a superb short novel. Bannadonna, "the great mechanician, the unblest foundling," seeking to conquer a larger liberty, like Prometheus, instead extended the empire of necessity. His great Bell-Tower, intended to be the noblest in Italy, survives only as "a stone pine," a "black massed stump." It is the new tower of Babel:

> Like Babel's, its base was laid in a high hour of renovated earth, following the second deluge, when the waters of the Dark Ages had dried up, and once more the green appeared. No wonder that, after so long and deep submersion, the jubilant expectation of the race should, as with Noah's sons, soar into Shinar aspiration.
>
> In firm resolve, no man in Europe at that period went beyond Bannadonna. Enriched through commerce with the Levant, the state in which he lived voted to have the noblest Bell-Tower in Italy. His repute assigned him to be architect.
>
> Stone by stone, month by month, the tower rose. Higher, higher; snail-like in pace, but torch or rocket in its pride.
>
> After the masons would depart, the builder, standing alone upon its ever-ascending summit, at close of every day, saw that he overtopped still higher walls and trees. He would tarry till a late hour there, wrapped in schemes of other and still loftier piles. Those who of saints' days thronged the spot — hanging to the rude poles of scaffolding, like sailors on

yards, or bees on boughs, unmindful of lime and dust, and falling chips of stone — their homage not the less inspirited him to self-esteem.

At length the holiday of the Tower came. To the sound of viols, the climax-stone slowly rose in air, and, amid the firing of ordnance, was laid by Bannadonna's hands upon the final course. Then mounting it, he stood erect, alone, with folded arms, gazing upon the white summits of blue inland Alps, and whiter crests of bluer Alps off-shore — sights invisible from the plain. Invisible, too, from thence was that eye he turned below, when, like the cannon booms, came up to him the people's combustions of applause.

That which stirred them so was, seeing with what serenity the builder stood three hundred feet in air, upon an unrailed perch. This none but he durst do. But his periodic standing upon the pile, in each stage of its growth — such discipline had its last result.

We recognize Captain Ahab in Bannadonna, though Ahab has his humanities, and the great mechanician lacks all pathos. Ahab plays out an avenger's tragedy, but Bannadonna's purpose lacks any motivation except pride. His pride presumably is related to the novelist's, and the black stump that is the sole remnant of the Bell-Tower might as well be *Pierre*, little as Melville would have welcomed such an identification. The sexual mortification of the image is palpable, yet adds little to the comprehensiveness of what will become Bannadonna's doom, since that necessarily is enacted as a ritual of castration anyway. Melville's Prometheans, Ahab and Bannadonna, have an overtly Gnostic quarrel with the heavens. Melville's narratives, at their strongest, know implicitly what Kafka asserted with rare explicitness in his great parable:

> The crows maintain that a single crow could destroy the heavens. Doubtless that is so, but it proves nothing against the heavens for the heavens signify simply: the impossibility of crows.

In Melville, the heavens signify simply: the impossibility of Ahab and of Bannadonna. Ahab is a hunter and not a builder, but to destroy Moby-Dick or to build the Bell-Tower would be to pile up the Tower of Babel and get away with it:

> If it had been possible to build the Tower of Babel without ascending it, the work would have been permitted.

Kafka's aphorism would be an apt title for Melville's story, with Bannadonna who has built his tower partly in order to ascend it and to stand "three hundred feet in air, upon an unrailed perch." Kafka could have told Bannadonna that a labyrinth underground would have been better, though of course that too would not have been permitted, since the heavens would have regarded it as the pit of Babel:

> What are you building? — I want to dig a subterranean passage. Some progress must be made. My station up there is much too high.
>   We are digging the pit of Babel.

Bannadonna is closest to the most extraordinary of the Kafkan parables concerning the Tower, in which a scholar maintains that the Great Wall of China "alone would provide for the first time in the history of mankind a secure foundation for the new Tower of Babel. First the wall, therefore, and then the tower." The final sentence of "The Great Wall and the Tower of Babel" could have impressed Melville as the best possible commentary upon Bannadonna-Melville, both in his project and his fate:

> There were many wild ideas in people's heads at that time — this scholar's book is only one example — perhaps simply because so many were trying to join forces as far as they could for the achievement of a single aim. Human nature, essentially changeable, unstable as the dust, can endure no restraint; if it binds itself it soon begins to tear madly at its bonds, until it rends everything asunder, the wall, the bonds and its very self.

The fall of Bannadonna commences with the casting of the great bell:

> The unleashed metals bayed like hounds. The workmen shrunk. Through their fright, fatal harm to the bell was dreaded. Fearless as Shadrach, Bannadonna, rushing through the glow, smote the chief culprit with his ponderous ladle. From the smitten part, a splinter was dashed into the seething mass, and at once was melted in.

That single blemish is evidently Melville's personal allegory for

whatever sense of guilt, in his own pained judgment, flawed his own achievement, even in *Moby-Dick*. More interesting is Bannadonna's creation of a kind of *golem* or Frankensteinean monster, charmingly called Haman, doubtless in tribute to the villain of the Book of Esther. Haman, intended to be the bell-ringer, is meant also "as a partial type of an ulterior creature," a titanic helot who would be called Talus, like the rather sinister iron man who wields an iron flail against the rebellious Irish in the savage book 5 of Spenser's *The Faerie Queene*. But Talus is never created; Haman is quite enough to immolate the ambitious artist, Bannadonna:

> And so, for the interval, he was oblivious of his creature; which, not oblivious of him, and true to its creation, and true to its heedful winding up, left its post precisely at the given moment; along its well-oiled route, slid noiselessly towards its mark; and, aiming at the hand of Una, to ring one clangorous note, dully smote the intervening brain of Bannadonna, turned backwards to it; the manacled arms then instantly up-springing to their hovering poise. The falling body clogged the thing's return; so there it stood, still impending over Bannadonna, as if whispering some post-mortem terror. The chisel lay dropped from the hand, but beside the hand; the oil-flask spilled across the iron track.

Which of his own works destroyed Melville? Juxtapose the story's deliberately Addisonian or Johnsonian conclusion with the remarkable stanza in Hart Crane's "The Broken Tower" that it helped inspire, and perhaps a hint emerges, since Crane was a superb interpreter of Melville:

> So the blind slave obeyed its blinder lord; but, in obedience, slew him. So the creator was killed by the creature. So the bell was too heavy for the tower. So that bell's main weakness was where man's blood had flawed it. And so pride went before the fall.

> > The bells, I say, the bells break down their tower;
> > And swing I know not where. Their tongues engrave
> > Membrane through marrow, my long-scattered score
> > Of broken intervals . . . And I, their sexton slave!

Crane is both Bannadonna and Haman, a complex fate darker even than Melville's, who certainly had represented himself as Bannadonna.

The Bell-Tower of Bannadonna perhaps was *Pierre* but more likely *Moby-Dick* itself, Melville's "long-scattered score / Of broken intervals" even as *The Bridge* was Hart Crane's. This is hardly to suggest that Haman is Captain Ahab. Yet Melville's "wicked book," as he called *Moby-Dick* in a famous letter to Hawthorne, indeed may have slain something vital in its author, if only in his retrospective consciousness.

Prologue to Herman Melville's "Bartleby"

Jorge Luis Borges

In the winter of 1851, Melville published *Moby-Dick*, the infinite novel which has decided his fame. Page by page, the narrative expands, to the point of usurping the magnitude of the cosmos. At the beginning, the reader may imagine that its theme is the wretched life of the whalers; then that the theme is the madness of Captain Ahab, eager to chase and to kill the White Whale; then that the whale and Ahab and the pursuit that wear out the earth's seas are symbols and mirrors of the Universe. In order to suggest that the book is symbolic, Melville declares, emphatically, that it is not: "Let no one consider Moby-Dick a monstrous fable, or what would be a hideous and intolerable allegory." (Characteristically, Borges shortens and alters Melville's text in order to mesh it with his own argument and syntax. The English text reads: "So ignorant are most landsmen of some of the plainest and most palpable wonders of the world, that without some hints touching the plain facts, historical and otherwise, of the fishery, they might scout at *Moby-Dick* as a monstrous fable, or still worse and more detestable, a hideous and intolerable allegory" [chapter 45] [Trans.].) The traditional connotation of the word "allegory" seems to have blinded the critics; they all choose to limit themselves to a moral interpretation of the work. Thus, E. M. Forster: "Narrowed and hardened into words the spiritual theme of *Moby-Dick* is as follows: a battle against evil conducted too long or in the wrong way." I agree, but the symbol of the whale is less apt for suggesting that the universe is vicious than for suggesting its vastness, its

From *Review: Latin American Literature and Art* 17 (Spring 1976). © 1976 by the Center for Inter-American Relations, Inc. Translated by Ronald Christ.

inhumanity, its bestial or enigmatic stupidity. In one of his stories, Chesterton compares the universe of the atheists to a labyrinth without a center. Such is the universe of *Moby-Dick:* a cosmos (a chaos) not only recognizably evil, as the Gnostics intuited, but irrational as well, like that in the hexameters of Lucretius.

Moby-Dick is written in a romantic dialect of English, an impassioned dialect that alternates or combines rhetorical schemes of Shakespeare and Thomas De Quincey, of Browne and Carlyle; "Bartleby" is written in a calm, even droll diction whose deliberate application to an infamous subject matter seems to prefigure Kafka. Nevertheless, between both fictions, there is a secret, central affinity. In the former, Ahab's monomania disturbs and finally destroys all the men on the boat (in translating Melville's novel into his own view of it, Borges ignores the survival of Ishmael, the narrator of *Moby-Dick* [trans.]) in the latter, Bartleby's frank nihilism contaminates his companions and even the stolid man who tells Bartleby's story, the man who pays him for his imaginary labors. It is as if Melville had written: "It is enough that one man is irrational for others to be irrational and for the universe to be irrational." The history of the universe teems with confirmations of this fear.

"Bartleby" belongs to the volume entitled *The Piazza Tales* (New York and London, 1856). About another narrative in that book, John Freeman observes that it could not be fully understood until Joseph Conrad published certain analogous works, almost half a century later. I would observe that the work of Kafka projects a curious, hind light on "Bartleby." "Bartleby" already defines a genre that Kafka would re-invent and quarry around 1919: the genre of fantasies of conduct and feeling or, as it is unfortunately termed today, the psychological. Beyond that, the opening pages of "Bartlby" do not foreshadow Kafka; rather, they allude to or repeat Dickens. . . . In 1849, Melville had published *Mardi,* an entangled and even unreadable novel, but one whose basic argument anticipates the obsessions and the mechanism of *The Castle, The Trial* and *Amerika:* it presents an infinite persecution across an infinite sea.

I have stated the affinities of Melville with other writers. I do not subordinate him to them; I am working under one of the laws of all description or definition: to compare the unknown to the known. Melville's greatness is substantial but his fame is new. Melville died in 1891; twenty years after his death, the eleventh edition of the *Encyclopedia Britannica* considers him a mere chronicler of life at sea; Lang and George Saintsbury, in 1922 and 1914, completely ignore him in their histories of English literature. Later, Lawrence of Arabia and D. H. Lawrence, Waldo Frank and Lewis

Mumford defended him. In 1921, Raymond Weaver published the first American monograph: *Herman Melville, Mariner and Mystic;* in 1926, John Freeman, the critical biography *Herman Melville.*

The enormous population, the tall cities, misleading and boisterous publicity have conspired to make great, secret men one of America's traditions. Edgar Allan Poe was one of them; Melville another.

$\mathbf{M}$elville's Parable of the Walls

Leo Marx

> *Dead,*
> > *25. Of a wall . . .: Unbroken, unrelieved by breaks or interruptions; absolutely uniform and continuous.*
> > New English Dictionary

In the spring of 1851, while still at work on *Moby-Dick*, Herman Melville wrote his celebrated "dollars damn me" letter to Hawthorne:

> In a week or so, I go to New York, to bury myself in a third-story room, and work and slave on my "Whale" while it is driving through the press. *That* is the only way I can finish it now — I am so pulled hither and thither by circumstances. The calm, the coolness, the silent grass-growing mood in which a man *ought* always to compose, — that, I fear, can seldom be mine. Dollars damn me. . . . My dear Sir, a presentiment is on me, — I shall at last be worn out and perish. . . . What I feel most moved to write, that is banned, — it will not pay. Yet, altogether, write the *other* way I cannot.

He went on and wrote the "Whale" as he felt moved to write it; the public was apathetic and most critics were cool. Nevertheless Melville stubbornly refused to return to the *other* way, to his more successful earlier modes, the South Sea romance and the travel narrative. In 1852 he published *Pierre*, a novel even more certain not to be popular. And this time the critics were vehemently hostile. Then, the following year, Melville turned to shorter fiction. "Bartleby the Scrivener," the first of his stories, dealt with a problem

---

From *The Sewanee Review* 61, no. 4 (Autumn 1953). © 1953, renewed 1981 by the University of the South.

unmistakably like that Melville had described to Hawthorne.

There are excellent reasons for reading "Bartleby" as a parable having to do with Melville's own fate as a writer. To begin with, the story *is* about a kind of writer, a "copyist" in a Wall Street lawyer's office. Furthermore, the copyist is a man who obstinately refuses to go on doing the sort of writing demanded of him. Under the circumstances there can be little doubt about the connection between Bartleby's dilemma and Melville's own. Although some critics have noted the autobiographical relevance of this facet of the story, a close examination of the parable reveals a more detailed parallel with Melville's situation than has been suggested. In fact the theme itself can be described in a way which at once establishes a more precise relation. "Bartleby" is not only about a writer who refuses to conform to the demands of society, but it is, more relevantly, about a writer who forsakes conventional modes because of an irresistible preoccupation with the most baffling philosophical questions. This shift of Bartleby's attention is the symbolic equivalent of Melville's own shift of interest between *Typee* and *Moby-Dick*. And it is significant that Melville's story, read in this light, does not by any means proclaim the desirability of the change. It was written in a time of deep hopelessness, and as I shall attempt to show, it reflects Melville's doubts about the value of this recent work.

Indeed, if I am correct about what this parable means, it has immense importance, for it provides the most explicit and mercilessly self-critical statement of his own dilemma that Melville has left us. Perhaps it is because "Bartleby" reveals so much of his situation that Melville took such extraordinary pains to mask its meaning. This may explain why he chose to rely upon symbols which derive from his earlier work, and to handle them with so light a touch that only the reader who comes to the story after an immersion in the other novels can be expected to see how much is being said here. Whatever Melville's motive may have been, I believe it may legitimately be accounted a grave defect of the parable that we must go back to *Typee* and *Moby-Dick* and *Pierre* for the clues to its meaning. It is as if Melville had decided that the only adequate test of a reader's qualifications for sharing so damaging a self-revelation was a thorough reading of his own work.

I

"Bartleby the Scrivener" is a parable about a particular kind of writer's relations to a particular kind of society. The subtitle, "A Story of Wall Street," provides the first clue about the nature of the society. It is a commercial society, dominated by a concern with property and finance. Most of the action takes place in Wall Street. But the designation has a further meaning: as Melville describes the street it literally becomes a walled street. The walls are the controlling symbols of the story, and in fact it may be said that this is a parable of walls, the walls which hem in the meditative artist and for that matter every reflective man. Melville also explicitly tells us that certain prosaic facts are "indispensable" to an understanding of the story. These facts fall into two categories: first, details concerning the personality and profession of the narrator, the center of consciousness in this tale, and more important, the actual floor-plan of his chambers.

The narrator is a Wall Street lawyer. One can easily surmise that at this unhappy turning point in his life Melville was fascinated by the problem of seeing what his sort of writer looked like to a representative American. For his narrator he therefore chose, as he did in "Benito Cereno," which belongs to the same period, a man of middling status with a propensity for getting along with people, but a man of distinctly limited perception. Speaking in lucid, matter-of-fact language, this observer of Bartleby's strange behavior describes himself as comfortable, methodical and prudent. He has prospered; he unabashedly tells of the praise with which John Jacob Astor has spoken of him. Naturally, he is a conservative, or as he says, an "eminently *safe*" man, proud of his snug traffic in rich men's bonds, mortgages and deeds. As he tells the story we are made to feel his mildness, hs good humor, his satisfaction with himself and his way of life. He is the sort who prefers the remunerative though avowedly obsolete sinecure of the Mastership of Chancery, which has just been bestowed upon him when the action starts, to the exciting notoriety of the courtroom. He wants only to be left alone; nothing disturbs his complacency until Bartleby appears. As a spokesman for the society he is well chosen; he stands at its center and performs a critical role, unravelling and retying the invisible cords of property and equity which intertwine in Wall Street and bind the social system.

The lawyer describes his chambers with great care, and only when the plan of the office is clearly in mind can we find the key to the parable. Although the chambers are on the second floor, the surrounding buildings rise above them, and as a result only very limited vistas are presented to those inside the office. At each end the windows look out upon a wall. One of the walls, which is part of a sky-light shaft, is *white*. It provides the best light available, but even from the windows which open upon the white wall the sky is invisible. No direct rays of the sun penetrate the legal sanctum. The wall at the other end gives us what seems at first to be a sharply contrasting view of the outside world. It is a lofty brick structure within ten feet of the lawyer's window. It stands in an everlasting shade and is *black* with age; the space it encloses reminds the lawyer of a huge black cistern. But we are not encouraged to take this extreme black and white, earthward and skyward contrast at face value (readers of *Moby-Dick* will recall how illusory colors can be), for the lawyer tells us that the two "views," in spite of their colors, have something very important in common: they are equally "deficient in what landscape painters call 'life.'" The difference in color is less important than the fact that what we see through each window is only a wall.

This is all we are told about the arrangement of the chambers until Bartleby is hired. When the lawyer is appointed Master in Chancery he requires the services of another copyist. He places an advertisement, Bartleby appears, and the lawyer hastily checks his qualifications and hires him. Clearly the lawyer cares little about Bartleby's previous experience; the kind of writer wanted in Wall Street need merely be one of the great interchangeable white-collar labor force. It is true that Bartleby seems to him peculiarly pitiable and forlorn, but on the other hand the lawyer is favorably impressed by his neat, respectable appearance. So sedate does he seem that the boss decides to place Bartleby's desk close to his own. This is his first mistake; he thinks it will be useful to have so quiet and apparently tractable a man within easy call. He does not understand Bartleby then or at any point until their difficult relationship ends.

When Bartleby arrives we discover that there is also a kind of wall inside the office. It consists of the ground-glass folding-doors which separate the lawyer's desk, and now Bartleby's, from the desks of the other employees, the copyists and the office boy. Unlike the walls outside the windows, however, this is a social barrier men can cross, and the lawyer makes a point of telling us that he opens and shuts these doors according to *his* humor. Even when they are shut, it should be noted, the ground glass provides at least an illusion of penetrability quite different from the opaqueness of the walls outside.

So far we have been told of only two possible views of the external world which are to be had from the office, one black and the other white. It is fitting that the coming of a writer like Bartleby is what makes us aware of another view, one neither black nor white, but a quite distinct third view which is now added to the topography of the Wall Street microcosm.

I placed his desk close up to a small side-window in that part of the room [a corner near the folding-doors] — a window which originally had afforded a lateral view of certain grimy back yards and bricks, but which, owing to subsequent erections, commanded at present no view at all, though it gave some light. Within three feet of the panes was a wall, and the light came down from far above, between two lofty buildings, as from a very small opening in a dome. Still further to a satisfactory arrangement, I procured a high green folding screen, which might entirely isolate Bartleby from my sight, though not remove him from my voice. And thus, in a manner, privacy and society were conjoined.

Notice that of all the people in the office Bartleby is to be in the best possible position to make a close scrutiny of a wall. His is only three feet away. And although the narrator mentions that the new writer's window offers "no view at all," we recall that he has, paradoxically, used the word "view" a moment before to describe the walled vista to be had through the other windows. Actually every window in the office looks out upon some sort of wall; the important difference between Bartleby and the others is that he is closest to a wall. Another notable difference is implied by the lawyer's failure to specify the color of Bartleby's wall. Apparently it is almost colorless, or blank. This also enhances the new man's ability to scutinize and know the wall which limits his vision; he does not have to contend with the illusion of blackness or whiteness. Only Bartleby faces the stark problem of perception presented by the walls. For him external reality thus takes on some of the character it had for Ishmael, who knew that color did not reside in objects, and therefore saw beyond the deceptive whiteness of the whale to "a colorless, all-color of atheism." As we shall see, only the nature of the wall with which the enigmatic Bartleby is confronted can account for his strange behavior later.

What follows (and it is necessary to rememaber that all the impressions we receive are the lawyer's) takes place in three consecutive movements: Bartleby's gradually stiffening resistance to the Wall Street routine, then a series of attempts by the lawyer to enforce the scrivener's conformity, and finally, society's punishment of the recalcitrant writer.

During the first movement Bartleby holds the initiative. After he is hired he seems content to remain in the quasi-isolation provided by the "protective" *green* screen and to work silently and industriously. This screen, too, is a kind of wall, and its color, as will become apparent, means a great deal. Although Bartleby seems pleased with it and places great reliance upon it, the screen is an extremely ineffectual wall. It is the flimsiest of all the walls in and out of the office; it has most in common with the ground glass door — both are "folding," that is, susceptible to human manipulation.

Bartleby likes his job, and in fact at first seems the exemplar of the writer wanted by Wall Street. Like Melville himself in the years between *Typee* and *Pierre*, he is an ardent and indefatigable worker; Bartleby impresses the lawyer with probably having "been long famished for something to copy." He copies by sunlight and candlelight, and his employer, although he does detect a curiously silent and mechanical quality in Bartleby's behavior, is well satisfied.

The first sign of trouble is Bartleby's refusal to "check copy." It is customary for the scriveners to help each other in this dull task, but when Bartleby is first asked to do it, to everyone's astonishment, he simply says that he prefers not to. From the lawyer's point of view "to verify the accuracy of his copy" is an indispensable part of the writer's job. But evidently Bartleby is the sort of writer who is little concerned with the detailed accuracy of his work, or in any case he does not share the lawyer's standards of accuracy. This passage is troublesome because the words "verify accuracy" seem to suggest a latter-day conception of "realism." For Melville to imply that what the public wanted of him in 1853 was a kind of "realism" is not plausible on historical grounds. But if we recall the nature of the "originals" which the lawyer wants impeccably copied the incident makes sense. These documents are mortgages and title-deeds, and they incorporate the offical version of social (property) relations as they exist at the time. It occurs to the lawyer that "the mettlesome poet, Byron" would not have acceded to such a demand either. And like the revolutionary poet, Bartleby apparently cares nothing for "common usage" or "common sense" — a lawyer's way of saying that this writer does not want his work to embody a faithful copy of human relations as they are conceived in the Street.

After this we hear over and over again the reiterated refrain of Bartleby's nay-saying. To every request that he do something other than copy he replies with his deceptively mild, "I would prefer not to." He adamantly refuses to verify the accuracy of copy, or to run errands, or to do anything but write. But it is not until much later that the good-natured lawyer begins to grasp the seriousness of his employee's passive resistance. A number of things hinder his perception. For one thing he admits that he is put off by the writer's impassive mask (he expresses himself only in his work); this and the fact that there seems nothing "ordinarily human" about him saves Bartleby from being fired on the spot. Then, too, his business preoccupations constantly "hurry" the lawyer away from considering what to do about Bartleby. He has more important things to think about; and since the scrivener unobtrusively goes on working in his green hermitage, the lawyer continues to regard him as a "valuable acquisition."

On this typically pragmatic basic the narrator has become reconciled to Bartleby until, one Sunday, when most people are in church, he decides to stop at his office. Beforehand he tells us that there are several keys to this Wall Street world, four in fact, and that he himself has one, one of the other copyists has another, and the scrubwoman has the third. (Apparently the representative of each social stratum has its own key.) But there is a fourth key he cannot account for. When he arrives at the office, expecting it to be deserted, he finds to his amazement that Bartleby is there. (If this suggests, however, that Bartleby holds the missing key, it is merely an intimation, for we are never actually provided with explicit evidence that he does, a detail which serves to underline Melville's misgivings about Bartleby's conduct throughout the story.) After waiting until Bartleby has a chance to leave, the lawyer enters and soon discovers that the scrivener has become a permanent resident of his Wall Street chambers, that he sleeps and eats as well as works there.

At this strange discovery the narrator feels mixed emotions. On the one hand the effrontery, the vaguely felt sense that his rights are being subverted, angers him. He thinks his actual identity, manifestly inseparable from his property rights, is threatened. "For I consider that one . . . is somehow unmanned when he tranquilly permits his hired clerk to dictate to him, and order him away from his own premises." But at the same time the lawyer feels pity at the thought of this man inhabiting the silent desert that is Wall Street on Sunday. Such abject friendlessness and loneliness draws him, by the bond of common humanity, to sympathize with the horrible solitude of the writer. So horrible is this solitude that it provokes in his mind a premonitory image of the scrivener's "pale form . . . laid out, among uncaring strangers, in its shivering winding sheet." He is reminded of the many "quiet mysteries" of the man, and of the "long periods he would stand looking out, at his pale window behind the screen, upon the *dead brick wall*." The lawyer now is aware that death is somehow an important constituent of that no-color wall which comprises Bartleby's view of reality. After this we hear several times of the forlorn writer immobilized in a "*dead*-wall revery."

He is obsessed by the wall of death which stands between him and a more ample reality than he finds in Wall Street.

The puzzled lawyer now concludes that Bartleby is the victim of an "innate" or "incurable" disorder; he decides to question him, and if that reveals nothing useful, to dismiss him. But his efforts to make Bartleby talk about himself fail. Communication between the writer and the rest of Wall Street society has almost completely broken down. The next day the lawyer notices that Bartleby now remains permanently fixed in a "dead-wall revery." He questions the writer, who calmly announces that he has given up all writing. "And what is the reason?" asks the lawyer. "Do you not see the reason for yourself?" Bartleby enigmatically replies. The lawyer looks, and the only clue he finds is the dull and glazed look of Bartleby's eyes. It occurs to him that the writer's "unexampled diligence" in copying may have had this effect upon his eyes, particularly since he has been working near the dim window. (The light surely is very bad, since the wall is only three feet away.) If the lawyer is correct in assuming that the scrivener's vision has been "temporarily impaired" (Bartleby never admits it himself) then it is the proximity of the colorless dead-wall which has incapacitated him. As a writer he has become paralyzed by trying to work in the shadow of the philosophic problems represented by the wall. From now on Bartleby does nothing but stand and gaze at the impenetrable wall.

Here Melville might seem to be abandoning the equivalence he has established between Bartleby's history and his own. Until he chooses to have Bartleby stop writing and stare at the wall the parallel between his career as a writer and Bartleby's is transparently close. The period immediately following the scrivener's arrival at the office, when he works with such exemplary diligence and apparent satisfaction, clearly corresponds to the years after Melville's return to America, when he so industriously devoted himself to his first novels. And Bartleby's intransigence ("I prefer not to") corresponds to Melville's refusal ("Yet . . . write the *other* way I cannot.") to write another *Omoo*, or, in his own words, another "beggarly 'Redburn.'" Bartleby's switch from copying what he is told to copy to staring at the wall is therefore, presumably, the emblematic counterpart to that stage in Melville's career when he shifted from writing best-selling romances to a preoccupation with the philosophic themes which dominate *Mardi*, *Moby-Dick* and *Pierre*. But the question is, can we accept Bartleby's merely passive staring at the blank wall as in any sense a parallel to the state of mind in which Melville wrote the later novels?

The answer, if we recall who is telling the story, is Yes. This is the lawyer's story, and in his eyes, as in the eyes of Melville's critics and the public, this stage of his career *is* artistically barren; his turn to metaphysical themes *is* in fact the equivalent of ceasing to write. In the judgment of his contemporaries Melville's later novels are no more meaningful than Bartleby's absurd habit of staring at the dead-wall. Writing from the point of view of the Wall Street lawyer, Melville accepts the popular estimate of his work and of his life. The scrivener's trance-like stare is the surrealistic device with which Melville leads us into the nightmare world where he sees himself as his countrymen do. It is a world evoked by terror, and particularly the fear that he may have allowed himself to get disastrously out of touch with actuality. Here the writer's refusal to produce what the public wants is a ludicrous mystery. He loses all capacity to convey ideas. He becomes a prisoner of his own consciousness. "Bartleby the Scrivener" is an imaginative projection of that premonition of exhaustion and death which Melville had described to Hawthorne.

To return to the story. With his decision to stop copying the first, or "Bartleby," movement ends. For him writing is the only conceivable kind of action, and during the rest of his life he is therefore incapable of action or, for that matter, of making any choice except that of utter passivity. When he ceases to write he begins to die. He remains a fixture in the lawyer's chamber, and it is the lawyer who now must take the initiative. Although the lawyer is touched by the miserable spectacle of the inert writer, he is a practical man, and he soon takes steps to rid himself of the useless fellow.

He threatens Bartleby, but the writer cannot be frightened. He tries to bribe him, but money holds no appeal for Bartleby. Finally he conceives what he thinks to be a "masterly" plan; he will simply convey to the idle writer that he "assumes" Bartleby, now that he has ceased to be productive, will vacate the premises. But when he returns to the office after having communicated this assumption, which he characteristically thinks is universally acceptable, he finds Bartleby still at his window. This "doctrine of assumptions," as he calls it, fails because he and the writer patently share no assumptions whatsoever about either human behavior or the nature of reality. However, if Bartleby refuses to accept the premises upon which the Wall Street world operates, he also refuses to leave. We later see that the only escape available to Bartleby is by way of prison or death.

Bartleby stays on, and then an extraordinary thing happens. After yet another abortive attempt to communicate with the inarticulate

scrivener the narrator finds himself in such a state of nervous indignation that he is suddenly afraid he may murder Bartleby. The fear recalls
to his mind the Christian doctrine of charity, though he still tends, as
Melville's Confidence-Man does later, to interpret the doctrine according to self-interest: it pays to be charitable. However, this partial return
to a Christian view leads him on toward metaphysical speculation, and
it is here that he finds the help he needs. After reading Jonathan Edwards on the will and Joseph Priestley on necessity, both Christian
determinists (though one is a Calvinist and the other on the road to
Unitarianism), he becomes completely reconciled to his relationship
with Bartleby. He infers from these theologians that it is his fate to furnish Bartleby with the means of subsistence. This excursion in Protestant theology teaches him a kind of resignation; he decides to accept
the inexplicable situation without further effort to understand or
alleviate the poor scrivener's suffering.

At this point we have reached a stasis and the second, or "lawyer's"
movement ends. He accepts his relation to Bartleby as "some purpose of
an allwise Providence." As a Christian he can tolerate the obstinate
writer although he cannot help him. And it is an ironic commentary
upon this fatalistic explanation of what has happened that the lawyer's
own activities from now on are to be explicitly directed not, insofar as
the evidence of the story can be taken as complete, by any supernatural
force, but rather by the Wall Street society itself. Now it seems that it is
the nature of the social order which determines Bartleby's fate. (The
subtitle should be recalled; it is after all Wall Street's story too.) For the
lawyer admits that were it not for his professional friends and clients he
would have condoned Bartleby's presence indefinitely. But the
sepulchral figure of the scrivener hovering in the background of business
conferences causes understandable uneasiness among the men of the
Street. Businessmen are perplexed and disturbed by writers, particularly writers who don't write. When they ask Bartleby to fetch a paper and
he silently declines, they are offended. Recognizing that his reputation
must suffer, the lawyer again decides that the situation is intolerable. He
now sees that the mere presence of a writer who does not accept Wall
Street assumptions has a dangerously inhibiting effect upon business.
Bartleby seems to cast a gloom over the office, and more disturbing, his attitude implies a denial of all authority. Now, more clearly than before, the
lawyer is aware that Bartleby jeopardizes the sacred right of private property
itself, for the insubordinate writer in the end may "outlive" him and so "claim
possession . . .[of his office] by right of perpetual occupancy" (a wonderful

touch!). If this happens, of course, Bartleby's unorthodox assumptions rather than the lawyer's will eventually dominate the world of Wall Street. The lawyer's friends, by "relentless remarks," bring great pressure to bear upon him, and henceforth the lawyer is in effect an instrument of the great power of social custom, which forces him to take action against the nonconforming writer.

When persuasion fails another time, the only new strategem which the lawyer can conceive is to change offices. This he does, and in the process removes the portable green screen which has provided what little defense Bartleby has had against his environment. The inanimate writer is left "the motionless occupant of a naked room." However, it soon becomes clear to the lawyer that it is not so easy to abdicate his responsibility. Soon he receives a visit from a stranger who reports that the scrivener still inhabits the old building. The lawyer refuses to do anything further. But a few days later several excited person, including his former landlord, confront him with the news that Bartleby not only continues to haunt the building, but that the whole structure of Wall Street society is in danger of being undermined. By this time Bartleby's rebellion has taken on an explicitly revolutionary character: "Everyone is concerned," the landlord tells the lawyer, "clients are leaving the offices; some fears are entertained of a mob."

Fear of exposure in the public press now moves the lawyer to seek a final interview with the squatter. This time he offers Bartleby a series of new jobs. To each offer the scrivener says no, although in every case he asserts that he is "not particular" about what he does; that is, all the jobs are equally distasteful to him. Desperate because of his inability to frighten Bartleby's "immobility into compliance," the lawyer is driven to make a truly charitable offer: he asks the abject copyist to come home with him. (The problem of dealing with the writer gradually brings out the best in this complacent American.) But Bartleby does not want charity; he prefers to stay where he is.

Then the narrator actually escapes. He leaves the city, and when he returns there is word that the police have removed Bartleby to the Tombs as a vagrant. (He learns that even physical compulsion was unable to shake the writer's impressive composure, and that he had silently obeyed the orders of the police.) There is an official request for the lawyer to appear and make a statement of the facts. He feels a mixture of indignation and approval at the news. At the prison he finds Bartleby standing alone in the "inclosed grass-platted yards" silently facing a high wall. Renewing his efforts to get through to the writer, all the lawyer can elicit is a cryptic *"I know where I am."* A moment later Bartleby turns away and again takes up a position "fronting the dead-wall." The wall, with its deathlike character, completely engages Bartleby. Whether "free" or imprisoned he has no concern for anything but the omnipresent and impenetrable wall. Taking the last resort of the "normal" man, the lawyer concludes that Bartleby is out of his mind.

A few days pass and the lawyer returns to the Tombs only to find that they have become, for Bartleby, literally a tomb. He discovers the wasted figure of the writer huddled up at the base of a wall, dead, but with his dim eyes open.

In a brief epilogue the lawyer gives us a final clue to Bartleby's story. He hears a vague report which he asserts has a "certain suggestive interest"; it is that Bartleby had been a subordinate clerk in the Dead Letter Office at Washington. There is some reason to believe, in other words, that Bartleby's destiny, his appointed vocation in this society, had been that of a writer who handled communications for which there were no recipients—PERSON UNKNOWN AT THIS ADDRESS. The story ends with the lawyer's heartfelt exclamation of pity for Bartleby and humankind.

II

What did Melville think of Bartleby? The lawyer's notion that Bartleby was insane is of course not to be taken at face value. For when the scrivener says that he knows where he is we can only believe that he does, and the central irony is that there was scarcely a difference, so far as the writer's freedom was concerned, between the prison and Wall Street. In Wall Street Bartleby did not read or write or talk or go anywhere or eat any dinners (he refuses to eat them in prison too) or, for that matter, do anything which normally would distinguish the free man from the prisoner in solitary confinement. And, of course, the office in which he had worked was enclosed by walls. How was this to be distinguished from the place where he died?

> The yard was entirely quiet. It was not accessible to the common prisoners. The surrounding walls, of amazing thickness, kept off all sounds behind them. The Egyptian character of the masonry weighed upon me with its gloom. But a soft imprisoned turf grew under foot. The heart of the eternal pyramids, it seemed, wherein, by some strange magic, through the clefts, grass-seed, dropped by the birds, had sprung.

At first glance the most striking difference between the Wall Street office and the prison is that here in prison there are four walls, while only three had been visible from the lawyer's windows. On reflection, however, we recall that the side of the office containing the door, which offered a kind of freedom to the others, was in effect a fourth wall for Bartleby. He had refused to walk through it. The plain inference is that he acknowledged no distinction between the lawyer's chambers and the world outside; his problem was not to be solved by leaving the office, or by leaving Wall Street; indeed, from Bartleby's point of view, Wall Street *was* America. The difference between Wall Street and the Tombs was an illusion of the lawyer's, not Bartleby's. In the prison yard, for example, the lawyer is disturbed because he thinks he sees, through the slits of the jail windows, the "eyes of murderers and thieves" peering at the dying Bartleby. (He has all along been persuaded of the writer's incorruptible honesty.) But the writer knows where he is, and he offers no objection to being among thieves. Such minor distinctions do not interest him. For him the important thing is that he still fronts the same dead-wall which has always impinged upon his consciousness, and upon the mind of the man since the beginning of time. (Notice the archaic Egyptian character of the prison wall.) Bartleby has come as close to the wall as any man can hope to do. He finds that it is absolutely impassable, and that it is not, as the Ahabs of the world would like to think, merely a pasteboard mask through which man can strike. The masonry is of "amazing thickness."

Then why has Bartleby allowed the wall to paralyze him? The others in the office are not disturbed by the walls; in spite of the poor light they are able to do their work. Is it possible that Bartleby's suffering is, to some extent, self-inflicted? that it is symptomatic of the perhaps morbid fear of annihilation manifested in his preoccupation with the dead-wall? Melville gives us reason to suspect as much. For Bartleby has come to regard the walls as permanent, immovable parts of the structure of things, comparable to man's inability to surmount the limitations of his sense perceptions, or comparable to death itself. He has forgotten to take account of the fact that these particular walls which surround the office are, after all, man-made. They are products of society, but he has imputed eternality to them. In his disturbed mind metaphysical problems which seem to be timeless concomitants of the condition of man and problems created by the social order are inextricably joined, joined in the symbol of the wall.

And yet, even if we grant that Bartleby's tortured imagination has had a part in creating his dead-wall, Melville has not ignored society's share of responsibility for the writer's fate. There is a sense in which Bartleby's state of mind may be understood as a response to the hostile world of Wall Street. Melville has given us a fact of the utmost importance: the window through which Bartleby had stared at the wall had "originally . . . afforded a lateral view of certain grimy backyards and bricks, but . . . owing to subsequent erections, commanded at present no view at all, though it gave some light." Melville's insinuation is that the wall, whatever its symbolic significance for Bartleby, actually served as an impediment to (or substitute for?) the writer's vision of the world around him. This is perhaps the most awesome moment in Melville's cold self-examination. The whole fable consists of a surgical probing of Bartleby's motives, and here he questions the value, for a novelist, of those metaphysical themes which dominate his later work. What made Bartleby turn to the wall? There is the unmistakable hint that such themes (fixing his attention on "subsequent erections") had had the effect of shielding from view the sordid social scene ("grimy backyards and bricks") with which Melville, for example, had been more directly concerned in earlier novels such as *Redburn* or *White-Jacket*. At this point we are apparently being asked to consider whether Bartleby's obsession was perhaps a palliative, a defense against social experience which had become more than he could stand. To this extent the nature of the Wall Street society has contributed to Bartleby's fate. What is important here, however, is that Melville does not exonerate the writer by placing all the onus upon society. Bartleby has made a fatal mistake.

Melville's analysis of Bartleby's predicament may be appallingly detached, but it is by no means unsympathetic. When he develops the contrast between a man like Bartleby and the typical American writers of his age there is no doubt where his sympathies lie. The other copyists in the office accept their status as wage earners. The relations between them are tinged by competitiveness — even their names, "Nippers" and "Turkey," suggest "nip and tuck." Nevertheless they are not completely satisfactory employees; they are "useful" to the lawyer only half of the time. During half of each day each writer is industrious and respectful and compliant; during the other half he tends to be recalcitrant and even mildly rebellious. But fortunately for their employer these half-men are never aggressive at the same time, and so he easily dominates them, he compels them to do the sort of writing he wants, and has them "verify the accuracy" of their work according to his standard. When Bartleby's resistance begins they characteristically waver between him and the lawyer. Half the time, in their "submissive" moods ("submission" is their favorite word as "prefer" is Bartleby's), they stand with the employer and are incensed against Bartleby, particularly when his resistance inconveniences *them*; the rest of the time they mildly approve of his behavior, since it expresses their own ineffectual impulses toward independence. Such are the writers the society selects and, though not too lavishly, rewards.

One of Melville's finest touches is the way he has these compliant and representative scriveners, though they never actually enlist in Bartleby's cause, begin to echo his "prefer" without being aware of its source. So does the lawyer. "Prefer" is the nucleus of Bartleby's refrain, "I prefer not to," and it embodies the very essence of his power. It simply means "choice," but it is backed up, as it clearly is not in the case of the other copyists, by will. And it is in the stength of his will that the crucial difference between Bartleby and other writers lies. When Nippers and Turkey use the word "prefer" it is only because they are unconsciously imitating the manner, the surface vocabulary of the truly independent writer; they say "prefer," but in the course of the parable they never make any real choices. In their mouths "prefer" actually is indistinguishable from "submission"; only in Bartleby's does it stand for a genuine act of will. In fact writers like Nippers and Turkey are incapable of action, a trait carefully reserved for Bartleby, the lawyer, and the social system itself (acting through various agencies, the lawyers' clients, the landlord, and the police). Bartleby represents the only real, if ultimately ineffective, threat to society; his experience gives some support to Henry Thoreau's view that one lone intransigent man can shake the foundations of our institutions.

But he can only shake them, and in the end the practical consequence of Bartleby's rebellion is that society has eliminated an enemy. The lawyer's premonition was true; he finally sees Bartleby in death. Again the story insinuates the most severe self-criticism. For the nearly lifeless Bartleby, attracted neither by the skyward tending white wall, nor the cistern-like black wall, had fixed his eyes on the "dead" wall. This wall of death which surrounds us, and which Melville's heroes so desperately needed to pierce, has much in common with the deadly White Whale. Even Ahab, who first spoke of the whale as a "pasteboard mask" through which man might strike, sensed this, and he significantly shifted images in the middle of this celebrated quarter-deck reply to Starbuck:

All visible objects, man, are, but as pasteboard masks. . . . If man will strike, strike through the mask! How can the

prisoner reach outside, except by thrusting through the wall?
To me, the white whale is that wall, shoved near to me.

Like the whale, the wall will destroy the man who tries too obstinately to
penetrate it. Bartleby had become so obsessed by the problem of the
dead-wall that his removal to prison hardly changed his condition, or,
for that matter, the state of his being; even in the walled street he had
allowed his life to become suffused by death.

The detachment with which Melville views Bartleby's situation is
perhaps the most striking thing about the fable. He gives us a powerful
and unequivocal case against Wall Street society for its treatment of the
writer, yet he avoids the temptation of finding in social evil a sentimental sanction for everything his hero thinks and does. True, the society
has been indifferent to Bartleby's needs and aspirations; it has demanded of him a kind of writing he prefers not to do; and, most serious of all,
it has impaired his vision by forcing him to work in the shadow of its
walls. Certainly society shares the responsibility for Bartleby's fate. But
Melville will not go all the way with those who find in the guilt of society
an excuse for the writer's every hallucination. To understand what led to
Bartleby's behavior is not to condone it. Melville refuses to ignore the
painful fact that even if society shares the blame for Bartleby's delusion,
it was nevertheless a delusion. What ultimately killed this writer was not
the walls themselves, but the fact that he confused the walls built by men
with the wall of human mortality.

III

Is this, then, as F. O. Matthiessen has written, "a tragedy of utter
negation"? If it is not it is because there is a clear if muted note of affirmation here which must not be ignored. In the end, in prison, we are
made to feel that the action has somehow taken us closer to the
mysterious source of positive values in Melville's universe. "And see,"
says the lawyer to Bartleby in the prison yard, "it is not so sad a place as
one might think. Look, there is the sky, and here is the grass." To the
lawyer the presence of the grass in the Tombs is as wonderful as its
presence in the heart of eternal pyramids where "by some strange magic
through the clefts, grass-seed, dropped by birds, had sprung." The saving
power attributed to the green grass is the clue to Melville's affirmation.

The green of the grass signifies everything that the walls, whether
black or white or blank, do not. Most men who inhabit Wall Street

merely accept the walls for what they are — man-made structures which compartmentalize experience. To Bartleby, however, they are abstract emblems of all the impediments to man's realization of his place in the universe. Only the lawyer sees that the outstanding characteristic of the walls, whether regarded as material objects or as symbols, is that they are "deficient in . . . 'life.'" Green, on the other hand, *is* life. The color green is the key to a cluster of images of fecundity which recurs in Melville's work beginning with *Typee*. It is the color which dominates that tropical primitive isle. It is the color of growth and of all pastoral experience. Indeed the imminent disappearance of our agrarian society is an important motive for Ishmael's signing on the Pequod. "Are the green fields gone?" he asks as *Moby-Dick* begins. And later he says, in describing the ecstacy of squeezing sperm: "I declare to you that for the time I lived as in a musky meadow." So he give a green tint to his redeeming vision of "attainable felicity," a felicity which he says resides in the country, the wife, the heart, the bed — wherever, that is, men may know the magical life-giving force in the world. And *Pierre,* published the year before "Bartleby," also begins with a vision of a green paradise. There Melville makes his meaning explicit. He compares a certain green paint made of verdigris with the "democratic element [which] operates as subtile acid among us, forever producing new things by corroding the old."

> Now in general nothing can be more significant of decay than the idea of corrosion; yet on the other hand, nothing can more vividly suggest luxuriance of life than the idea of green as a color; for green is the peculiar signet of all-fertile Nature itself.

By some curious quirk of the human situation, Bartleby's uncompromising resistance, which takes him to prison, also take him a step closer to the green of animal faith. Melville deftly introduces this note of hope by having the lawyer compare the grass in the prison yard to the mystery of the grass within the pyramids. In time greenness, the lawyer suggests, may penetrate the most massive of walls. Indeed green seems virtually inherent in time itself, a somehow eternal property of man's universe. And in a Wall Street society it is (paradoxically) most accessible to the scrivener when he finds himself in prison and at the verge of death. Why? If Bartleby's suicidal obsession has taken him closer to grass and sky, are we to understand that it has had consequences both heartening and meaningful? Is Melville implying, in spite of all the reasons he has given us for being skeptical of Bartleby's motives, that an understanding of his fate may show us the way to a genuine affirmation? Before attempting to answer these questions, it is appropriate to note here how remarkable a fusion of manner and content Melville has achieved. While the questions are never explicitly asked, they are most carefully insinuated. The unique quality of this tale, in fact, resides in its ability to say almost nothing on its placid and inscrutable surface, and yet so powerfully to suggest that a great deal is being said. This quality of style is a perfect embodiment of the theme itself: concealed beneath the apparently meaningless if not mad behavior of Bartleby is a message of utmost significance to all men.

While the presence of the grass at Bartleby's death scene is the clue to Melville's affirmation, the affirmation can only exist outisde of the scrivener's mind. Green now means nothing to him. In the Wall Street world he had known, the green fields *were* gone; he was able to see neither grass nor sky from the walled-in windows. The only green that remained was the artificial green painted upon his flimsy screen, the screen behind which he did his diligent early work. But the screen proved a chimerical means of protection. Again Melville seems to be pointing the most accusing questions at himself. Had not his early novels contained a strong ingredient of primitivism? Had he not in effect relied upon the values implicit in the *Typee* experience (values which reappeared in the image of the inaccessible "insular Tahiti" in *Moby-Dick*) as his shelter from the new America? Was this pastoral commitment of any real worth as a defense against a Wall Street society? The story of Bartleby and his green screen, like the letter to Hawthorne (dollars damn me!), denies that it was. In this fable, artificial or man-made green, used as a shield in a Wall Street office, merely abets self-delusion. As for the other green, the natural green of the grass in the prison yard, it is clear that Bartleby never apprehended its meaning. For one thing, a color could hardly have meant anything to him at that stage. His skepticism had taken him beyond any trust in the evidence of his senses; there is no reason to believe that green was for him any less illusory a color than the black or white of the walls. We know, moreover, that when he died Bartleby was still searching: he died with his eyes open.

It is not the writer but the lawyer, the complacent representative American, who is aware of the grass and to whom, therefore, the meaning is finally granted. If there is any hope indicated, it is hope for his, not Bartleby's, salvation. Recall that everything we understand of the scrivener's fate has come to us by way of the lawyer's consciousness. From the first the situation of the writer has been working upon the narrator's latent sensibility, gradually drawing upon his capacity for sympathy, his recognition of the bond between his desperate employee and the rest of mankind. And Bartleby's death elicits a cry of compassion from this man who had once grasped so little of the writer's problem. "Ah, Bartleby! Ah! humanity!" and his (and Melville's) last words. They contain the final revelation. Such deeply felt and spontaneous sympathy is the nearest equivalent to the green of the grass within reach of man. It is an expression of human brotherhood as persistent, as magical as the leaves of grass. Charity is the force which may enable men to meet the challenge of death, whose many manifestations, real and imagined, annihilated the valiant Bartleby.

The final words of the fable are of a piece with Melville's undeviating aloofness from his hero: they at once acknowledge Bartleby's courage and repudiate his delusion. If such a man as the lawyer is ultimately capable of this discernment, then how wrong Bartleby was in permitting the wall to become the exclusive object of his concern! The lawyer can be saved. But the scrivener, like Ahab, or one of Hawthorne's geniuses, has made the fatal error of turning his back on mankind. He has failed to see that there were in fact no impenetrable walls between the lawyer and himself. The only walls which had separated them were the folding (manipulatable) glass doors, and the green screen. Bartleby is wrong, but wrong or not, he is a hero; much as Ahab's mad quest was the necessary occasion for Ishmael's salvation, this writer's annihilation is the necessary occasion for Everyman's preception.

Among the countless imaginative statements of the artist's problems in modern literature, "Bartleby" is exceptional in its sympathy and hope for the average man, and in the severity of its treatment of the artist. This is particularly remarkable when we consider the seriousness of the rebuffs Melville had so recently been given by his contemporaries. But nothing, he is saying, may be allowed to relieve the writer of his obligations to mankind. If he forgets humanity, as Bartleby did, his art will die, and so will he. The lawyer, realizing this, at the last moment couples Bartleby's name with that of humanity itself. The fate of the artist is inseparable from that of all men. The eerie story of Bartleby is a compassionate rebuke to the self-absorption of the artist, and so a plea that he devote himself to keeping strong his bonds with the rest of mankind. Today, exactly a century after it was written, "Bartleby the Scrivener" is a counterstatement to the large and ever-growing canon of "ordealist" interpretations of the situation of the modern writer.

"Certain Phenomenal Men": The Example of *Billy Budd*

Warner Berthoff

> *"Ah, who can say what passes between people in such a relation?"*
> HENRY JAMES, *The Golden Bowl*

In the case of *Billy Budd* it may be well to ask at the start just what kind of performance we are dealing with. First of all, it is a narrated story— whatever else we may say of it must take account of the particular manner of its telling, More precisely, it is, in Melville's own phrase, "an inside narrative"; we are to take it as decisively identifying the characters and events it describes, so far as this may ever by done. It is of course an extraordinary poignant narrative, and one which many readers have felt to be extraordinarily meaningful. The difficulty, to judge from what has been written about it, comes in trying to say what exactly does happen in it and what the meaning is. A great deal of Melville's work, early and late, seems often to have an unsettling effect on the judgements of his readers, not least the more responsive and sympathetic among them. His writing has proved perilously attractive to certain extravagant fashions in present-day criticism, especially that of appealing to a few chosen works of literature for moral or even religious authority; or of imputing systems of meaning such as could not practically be secured within the actual form and scope of the work in question. The warping that results is not unnatural and may indeed express an unusual generosity of response; we all are drawn, in the flush of our involvement

From *The Example of Melville.* © 1962 by Princeton Univerity Press. Norton, 1972.

with some deeply stirring experience, to see it as containing come con-
clusive message or as delivering some consummate revelation of our
own earnest desiring. No claim of immunity in this respect is made for
the present account, which can only take its chances with the rest. . . .

The ground common to most discussion of *Billy Budd* is the assumption that the story is allegorical—a narrative representation of some
universal truth or law or balance of contraries, a parable of Good and Evil,
a reenactment of the Fall, a projected myth of a ritual killing which is also a
resurrection, and so on. Such interpretations do not have to be scrambled
for. The evidence they adduce is undeniably there. The trouble is rather
that the statement of them will seem to miss what one feels, as one reads
and rereads, to be the governing concentration and emphasis of the actual
telling. *Billy Budd* is indeed full of quickening intimations as to the larger,
the perhaps universal circumstance of human life—intimations which are
typical of Melville's imagination, as his explicitness in articulating them is
typical of his best performance as a writer. But the decisive narrative logic
and cogency of the story are, I think, to be found elsewhere. They are to be
found in an effort which Melville characteristically troubled to furnish
precise words for, the effort to "define and denominate certain phenomenal
men" (chap. 11). To render in force and detail through all the incident and
commentary of his narrative the essential feature and bearing of these
men, to name and make authoritative the example of character manifested
in them—this is what seems to me to lie at the heart of Melville's enterprise.
In *Billy Budd* he undertakes to define not universal truth but certain specific
and contingent examples of being and behavior.

This undertaking is not to be felt in equal force at every point in the
story. In the opening chapters a reader looking into *Billy Budd* for the
first time, without benefit of editorial introductions but with some
knowledge of Melville's earlier books, would be very likely to suppose
that he had come upon another *Israel Potter*. Melville (as a study of his
manuscript changes makes evident) had his difficulties in determining
the best use of his materials and in discovering the proper drift and consequence of his story. In some respects his problem, though on a different scale, resembles that of Hardy a few years later in the *The Dynasts:*
both works, looking back a century to the strange apocalyptic wars of a
long-vanished time, are not unconcerned with the particular ideological
issues of that time; yet both mean to place the ultimate causes and meaning of the events recorded in the working of less contingent forces. So
Billy Budd opens with several chapters on the historical background—the
war with revolutionary France, the naval mutinies—and repeatedly

turns aside to show how this bears upon the action. In fact, Melville goes further and introduces or intimates what might seem to be even more restrictive considerations, aligning Captain Vere (and himself as narrator) with a philosophic anti-Jacobinism, calling one ship the *Rights-of-Man* and another the *Athée,* and so forth. All this is clearly meant to inform the story. But it is not meant to explain the story. The historical circumstances touch on the story at every crisis but do not essentially determine it. We are to feel both elements, the framing conditions and the special action, as real and consequential; the era intensifies our sense of the event as the event substantiates our impression of the era; but each is to be apprehended as following its own logic. The trouble is that if we respond at all to the impressive terms and symbols Melville used to embody his story, we may press upon them too rigid or predetermined an arrangement; we may be misled (as E. M. Forster cautioned with regard to *Moby-Dick*) "into harmonizing the incidents" and so screen out the distinguishing "roughness and richness" of the narrative as a whole.

II

I do not mean to dismiss out of hand the various allegorical interpretations of *Billy Budd.* If only in their striking variety and equal conviction, they have much to tell us — about the nature of Melville's writing as well as about the excitements and hazards of criticism. No one has worked along this line of approach more discerningly than Professor Norman Holmes Pearson, whose findings have the merit of standing near the center of sensible opinion on the story and may serve briefly — I hope not unfairly — as a stalking horse. To Professor Pearson, *Billy Budd* is best understood by analogy to Milton's heroic poems: "What Melville was doing was to try to give in as universalized a way as possible . . . another redaction of the myth which had concerned Milton . . . in the trilogy of his three major works" — the Christian myth, that is, of the fall from innocence and the promise of redemption.

There are of course numerous particulars to support such an interpretation, and Professor Pearson and others have mustered them cogently; they need not be reviewed here. What does need to be said is commonplace enough: that the analogies Melville brings forward in support of his story — Billy as Adam, his hanging as a kind of Ascension, the yardarm as the True Cross, and so on — prove nothing in themselves about either his intention or his achievement. This is not simply because they are matched by an equal number of analogies of a quite different sort (so Billy, for example, is also compared to Apollo, to Hercules, to a Tahitian of Captain Cook's time courteously but indifferently receiving the ministrations of Christian missionaries, and to a St. Bernard dog). We are also to bear in mind that we are reading a nineteenth-century, not a seventeenth-century, writer; in Melville's time the literary apprehension of Christian myth was nearly as divorced from sacramental religion, and as merely moral and pathetic when not wholly sentimental, as the apprehension of classical myth. But in any case we need above all to look to the whole development of Melville's actual narrative and to the particular disposition and intensity of its insistences. The question is: how do all these evidences operate in the story? do they determine the action and constitute its first meaning? or are they at most a kind of illustrative commentary, suggesting by familiar analogy the appropriate pitch of feeling?

There is little doubt that Melville meant his story to be in some manner exemplary and that as he worked on it he found it profoundly moving; he "believed" in it. The strength of intimation in an inveterate explainer like Melville is in some proportion to the weight and spur of his own perplexities. The religious metaphors in *Billy Budd* do indeed confirm our sense of a religious depth in Melville's sensibility. But we must be wary of abstracting the stuff of these metaphors from his immediate deployment of them — the obvious temptation, but somehow especially insidious with this work. Melville himself is explicit about his procedures. Reaching the limit of observation and analysis in his presentation of John Claggart, he turns for a clinching notation to the Scriptural formula of the "mysteries of iniquity" (chap. 12). Now what he was trying to express seems to me sufficiently identified in that precisely climactic phrase, which perfectly secures his idea of the "something defective and abnormal" in the constitution of the master-at-arms. But Melville himself recognized and characteristically specified the risk he was taking in thus falling back, here and elsewhere, on the "lexicon of Holy Writ" in an age which had grown indifferent to it, which could no longer be relied on to understand all that might be involved in it. His caution is itself pointedly cautionary. For our time is not so much skeptical of religious doctrines and symbols — certainly not passionately and burdensomely skeptical as Melville was — as it is ignorant of them, which Melville was not. Perhaps the first truth about us in this respect is that we are the embarrassed receivers of (in Carlo Levi's phrase) a civilization which used to be Christian. We respect, we are in a civil way habituated to, the positions of Christian belief; but the norms of our experience no longer reinforce them. And finding in a document like

Billy Budd that this half-forgotten vocabulary has been restored to use, we may be overimpressed, mistaking mere unembarrassed familiarity with it for a reconstitution of its prime significance. But to make of *Billy Budd* an attempt, and an attempt comparable to Milton's, to reanimate the Christian myth of human destiny under divine law is to respond less to the limiting and authenticating particulars of Melville's story than to the pathos of its corroborative analogies and allusions, or perhaps to the transferred pathos of our own progressive disregard of them. Also it is to claim for Melville the kind of positive testament or settled belief which seems inconsistent with what we know of him; which all his tenacity in doubt, his frank and courageous ignorance, his respect for the discomforts of truth and the phenomenal ambiguities of existence, would have gone to keep him from taking refuge in, even for the space of a story, even at the end of his life.

No, the actual telling of *Billy Budd* will not bear so grand a burden of meaning, and was not intended to. What its limiting circumstances are, Melville is concerned to say as precisely as he can. His use of the military setting in constraint of the events of his story is to the point here. The martial law by which Billy goes to his death is usually held to be symbolic of some universal law or authority, such as divine providence: I think mistakenly. Nor can I follow Professor Richard Chase in comparing it with the "abstract legality" confronted by Antigone or the "inhumanly enforced legality" of *The Winter's Tale*; for the official agencies of justice in these plays are to be understood as wrong precisely in that, being "abstract" and "inhuman," they are other than what they ought to be. But Melville is at some pains to present the martial law as morally *sui generis*, and in its own terms morally unimpeachable. It is designed, he reminds us, solely to subserve the extraordinary circumstance of war. It is "War's child," as Captain Vere tells the court, and must of its nature look "but to the frontage, the appearance" of things — and not wrongly. As against moral or divine law it can have no regard to questions of motive or judgments of virtue: "The prisoner's deed — with that alone we have to do." It is for this terrible eventuality alone, otherwise it would be indefensible. But in the circumstances Melville sets out, there is no appeal from it.

Why Melville's story rides so easily in this rigid context, and what it gains from it, are absorbing questions, but beyond the compass of the present essay. My point now is simply that in *Billy Budd* martial law and the "military necessity" are accepted in their own right, without ulterior design. Melville does not choose, as he did in *White-Jacket*, to judge the martial discipline by a higher moral law; he makes such a standard available neither to Vere and the court in their search for the right action (though they reach out to it) nor to the reader in judging what has happened. Christian conscience, mercy, the judgment of God—these are neither directly opposed to martial law nor put aside as meaningless. Melville has Vere speak of such considerations as having the force of "Nature" in the hearts of men but as being, in the "singular" given case, inapplicable. Doctrines of Christianity are invoked in full support of the pathos of the story, but assent to them is not what is at stake. It interested Melville, indeed it profoundly moved him, to point out in passing how one part of his narrative seemed to confirm the Calvinist doctrine of depravity or how another suggested the "heresy" of natural innocence, but these propositions are not, as such, his subject or argument. The whole movement of suggestion in Melville's narrative seems to me the reverse of allegorical; the words and names for the action of the story, the thoughts and analogies that help define it, follow from it and are subject to it. The image of the action itself, or a particular occurrence involving particular persons, stands first.

In *Billy Budd* this image is constituted first of all by the three main characters, and the action proceeds from the capacity of spirit painstakingly attributed to each of them. Each is set before us as a kind of natural force; in fact Melville's probing curiosity projects what might seem a thoroughly deterministic explanation of their behavior if it was not so clearly in the service of a stubborn and wondering sense of their free agency. "Character" is in general rather curiously exhibited here, Melville's language repeatedly suggesting that it is best apprehended at any given moment by a kind of *savoring*. A man's character derives from the accumulated conditions (the seasonings, so to speak) of his whole life, and so registers as a "taste" or "flavor" on the "moral palate," as though too subtly compounded for stricter definition. It may be that no sequence of dramatic events will wholly communicate this distinguishing savor of character; the necessities of action, in art as in life, show little enough respect for persons. But the mode of exposition Melville turned to has other resources than dramatization, other ways of declaring its meanings. So the climax of this minutely specifying narration is reached in an episode in which the actual event is withheld, and we are referred instead to the *character* of the participants.

This is the episode in which, the trial over, Vere privately tells Billy the court's decision. Given in very nearly the shortest chapter of the narrative (chap. 23), it follows the longest and most detailed; and in contrast to the thorough exposition just concluded (of Vere's distress, the hesitant proceedings of the court, the ambiguities of the evidence, and all Vere's patient argument) it moves instead by conjecture and reticence. "Beyond the communication of the sentence," the main section of it begins, "what took place at this interview was never known." Yet on this elliptical passage the full weight of the narrative, accelerating after its slow-paced beginnings into the drama of the middle chapters, centers and falls, its steady simple movement coming full stop. By working so sensible a change of pace and manner, and by explicitly likening the hidden event to what must happen wherever in the world the circumstances are "at all akin to those here attempted to be set forth," Melville appears for the moment to be concentrating our attention on the very heart of his whole conception. What we are told is what it chiefly concerns him to have us know — the phenomenal quality of character in his two heroes. In their essential being Vere and Billy are as one, "each radically sharing in the rarer qualities of our nature — so rare indeed as to be all but incredible to average minds however much cultivated." On this basis and in these limited terms the narrator will risk "some conjectures." But insofar as his conjecture does accord with the rarity of spirit by which he has identified his protagonists, it may lead into the profoundest truth, it may be definitive.

So the chapter's central paragraph begins: "It would have been in consonance with the spirit of Captain Vere." The capacity of spirit being known, the weight and bearing of the event may be measured and its meaning grasped. And what capacity of spirit Melville meant to set before us begins to be confirmed in the virtues he gravely imagines as "not improbably" brought into play in the interview: in Vere, utter frankness and unselfishness, making him confess his own part in Billy's sentencing, and intensifying into the compassion of a father; in Billy an equal frankness, and bravery of course, but also joy, in the realization of his Captain's extraordinary trust. Yet these impressive virtues are in a way incidental. What draws the narrator on is the magnitide of the capability they speak for. Translated out of their customary stations, Vere and Billy meet as "two of great Nature's nobler order." Their entire competence of spirit before the event is assumed; only the immediate exercise of it goes past saying. Though the narration here makes a show of drawing back even from conjecture, the quality and the significance of the action continue to be defined; exact terms are used. Melville writes that "there is no telling the sacrament" when two such spirits embrace, but the very word "sacrament" precisely advances his explanation. The same tactic directs the closing sentence of this astonishing paragraph:

"There is privacy at the time, inviolable to the survivor, and holy oblivion, the sequel to each diviner magnanimity, providentially covers all at last." Here again the withholding is according to the inmost nature of that which is being disclosed; the "privacy" of the scene is a consequence of the great and rare virtue, the "magnanimity," at work in it.

May we not take this explanation, and the word that thus concludes it, as literally as we can? As with martial law, Melville's purpose was not to universalize the particular phenomenon, the capacity of spirit generating this encounter, but simply to identify it, to declare it in its own name. In Vere and Billy, the passage affirms, we have to do with magnanimity, with greatness of soul, a quality which, though "all but incredible to average minds however much cultivated," is nevertheless according to nature, and is touched with divinity — or whatever in human conduct is suggestive of divinity. Though it is constrained by Claggart's depravity of spirit (also "according to nature") and has still to undergo the pitiless operation of the "military necessity," this greatness of soul in the two heroes achieves in the sacrament of their coming together an "inviolable," a "diviner" magnanimity. As there is a mystery of iniquity in Claggart, there is a mystery of magnanimity in these two. It is given no power to prevent the now settled outcome of the action. Yet its radiance is beyond catastrophe. It is such as can survive those decisive accidents of individual existence — age, health, station, luck, particular experience — which Melville consistently presented the lives of his characters as being determined by. Now the narrative has come to its defining climax. Here the tone is set for what remains to be told, and not at the pitch of tragedy — the tone of exalted acceptance and muted patient joy which will be heard in the account of Billy in irons like a "slumbering child," in Billy's "God bless Captain Vere!" in Vere's dying with Billy's name on his lips (not in remorse, Melville specifies), and finally, and with what sure art, in the gravely acquiescent music of the closing ballad.

III

This view of the action of *Billy Budd* (a view not discouraged by the dedication to the "great heart" of Jack Chase) does not, I think, deny the story any power of suggestion or degree of achievement. Perhaps it may remove the sense of disproportion between theme and occasion which Professor Pearson's and kindred readings leave us with, yet at the same time increase the interest of Melville's actual accomplishment. For an idea of some fulfilled greatness of soul lies, as we know, at the center not only of classical tradition in moral philosophy and literature but of Christian tradition as well. It lies also (as securely as ideas of equality and civil liberty) at the heart of the democratic ethos. The great-souled man — what significant reckoning of our duty and destiny, whether in the mode of tragedy or satire or prophecy or simple witness, does not somehow take account of him? For what else do we especially revere a Washington and a Lincoln, whose unique place in the national pantheon is surely something more than the sum of their historical deeds? And what more momentous question can be put to the democratic writer than the question of greatness of mind and spirit in a mass society?

To follow out this view of the story might well lead into discussion of Melville's "Americanism," an absorbing matter certainly, though at present rather shopworn. Just as usefully it may lead us back to a parallel which I have made some point here of questioning — the example of Milton. The Milton who matters here, however, is not the Christian poet of paradise lost and regained but the prideful humanist whose dedication to the idea of magnanimity is proverbial in English letters. Milton's concern with this virtue in his writings, and his explicit pride in the pursuit of it in his life, are in fact foremost among the qualities which have given him his peculiar personal aura and earned him so much gratuitous personal hostility in our own anti-heroic times. They are also of the essence of his Protestantism, and it is not likely to be altogether accidental that the two writers of epic imagination and enterprise in the Protestant camp (if we may imagine one) of Anglo-American literature should show a common concern, a considered preoccupation, with magnanimity.

As we might expect, Milton was confident and unembarrassed in deploying the term. He used it consistently and (according to his lights) precisely, to denote a summary condition of virtuousness in which the lesser particular virtues were gathered up and lifted to grandeur; in this he followed the Aristotelian definition of magnanimity as the "crowning ornament" of the virtuous character (*Nicomachean Ethics*, 4, 3, 16). What is especially Miltonic is his emphasis on rational self-consciousness in the exercise of magnanimity. For him the concept signifies the highest reach of that "pious and just honoring of ourselves" which is a duty of the virtuous man second only to love of God. Cultivation of magnanimity thus becomes the great end of education — so we find him saying in this famous and characteristic sentence: "I call therefore a compleat and generous Education that which fits a man to perform justly, skillfully, and magnanimously all the offices both private and public of Peace and War." But to describe the ideal education is to consider what end man was born for; and it is in the account of the creation of Adam that we come to the furthest reach of Milton's idea:

> There wanted yet the Master work, the end
> Of all yet don; a Creature who not prone
> And Brute as other Creatures, but endu'd
> With Sanctitie of Reason might erect
> His Stature, and upright with Front serene
> Govern the rest, self-knowing, and from thence
> Magnanimous to correspond with Heav'n.

In magnanimity, so conceived, natural creation rises to its sovereign beauty and fulfillment. Would any nineteenth-century transcendentalist or mystical democrat ever claim more than this for the instructed soul of man?

Of these associations some were still viable for Melville but not all. It was precisely a doctrinal confidence in what the great-souled man might "correspond with" that, two hundred years later, his intelligence despaired of. At the same time certain outwardly passive virtues like humility and disinterestedness had come to seem far more positive and potentially heroic than they had been to Milton in his time. So Melville could specify in Vere a "certain unaffected modesty of manhood" without diminishing his general "ascendancy of character" or his Miltonic readiness for all private and public offices of peace and war. It is still, however, a traditionally heroic image of magnanimity that we are shown at the beginning of *Billy Budd* in the chapters on Nelson. Nelson's greatness in command is assumed; what concerned Melville was his personal behavior at Trafalgar and the charge of "vainglory" and "affectation" it lay open to. And though Melville was on the defensive here, he unequivocally championed the impulse of the great-hearted hero to display his greatness and love the glory of it. Given "a nature like Nelson" and the opportunity of a Trafalgar, then the "sort of priestly motive" that directed the great commander's conduct was, Melville insisted in one of his showiest sentences, altogether natural and fitting, coming from that "exaltation of sentiment" which is the mark of the truly heroic action.

The point is not that Milton's conception of magnanimity is a "source" of *Billy Budd*. What we are considering is not a case of "influence" but a comparable turn and reach of mind, formed in a broadly common moral tradition though expressing very different stages in its devolution. To Milton magnanimity was within the achieving of every wise and good man, a condition of completed moral being to be reached through rational procedures of education and piety. To Melville it was a rarer thing—much less a condition to be achieved, much more a mysterious distillation of certain transactions and contingencies in certain men's lives. At the high tide of his creative energy he could imagine it as naturally resulting from that "unshackled, democratic spirit of Christianity" in which America seemed destined to lead the world; we know how quickly this confidence went out of him. He found himself unable to assume even a moral efficacy in magnanimity, since he could not be sure in the first place of the moral order of creation, any more than he could have much faith in the moral justness of American society; both seemed paralyzingly indifferent to degrees of virtue. Nor could he take refuge in ideas of the infinitude of the private man or of the priesthood of the individual soul, as the simpler Protestant and democratic optimisms of his time would encourage him to. This being so, his undertaking in *Billy Budd*, and his success in it, are all the more impressive.

But did he in fact succeed? The character and role of Captain Vere fit well enough the traditional notion of magnanimity, but what about the character of Billy Budd? What has Miltonic magnanimity to do with the "mindless innocence" (as Professor Chase has put it) of the boy sailor? Given the character Melville presents, how much can be claimed for it? "To be bothing more than innocent!"—Claggart's "cynic disdain" may not be unreasonable; in one form or another it has been shared by most critics of the story. Have we not, in Billy, an expression of sentiment poignant in itself but unassimilated and unresolved in the narrative, and best explained (as Professor Chase would explain it) by the life-history and personal necessities of the author?

But magnanimity, we may note again, is not a substantive virtue. No particular actions prove it or follow from it. What the word describes is a certain dimension of spirit which the virtuous man may rise to and which any moral event may conceivably participate in. Whatever has a soul (and to Melville's excruciating animism anything can seem to) may in certain extraordinary circumstances grow into the condition of magnanimity, the soul that is called innocent not less than the soul instructed by experience. If innocence is compatible with virtuousness—and in characterizing Billy, Melville did not doubt that it is: "a virtue went out of him"—then it too is capable of its own kind of magnanimity.

Here again we may appeal to Melville's care to be explicit; for in working out his conception of the character of Billy Budd—a "child-man" not incapable of moral reflection yet mysteriously uncorrupted, able to conceive of death but like a savage warrior "wholly without irrational fear of it" — Melville does in fact "denominate" it categorically. This is in a passage of explanation added to chapter 16 of the revised draft, just after Billy has been approached by an apparent conspiracy of mutiny (though in his innocence he has hardly understood it as that). Melville, first specifying that the thought of reporting these overtures never entered Billy's mind, pushes on to a more positive claim, though at the moment a superfluous one: even if the step of reporting what he had heard *had* been suggested to him, "he would have been deterred from taking it by the thought, one of novice-magnanimity, that it would savor overmuch of the dirty work of a tell-tale." A special sort of magnanimity, awkwardly qualified and, though capable of choosing between evils, not yet decisively tested: nevertheless Melville makes it the defining motive in his conjecture here. Notice, too, that the term is introduced to attribute to Billy a natural revulsion from the role of informer; for in this he is sensibly at one with Captain Vere, who will respond to Claggart's accusations in the same way. To the magnanimous man, conscious of his nature and of the reputation it rightfully deserves, there may be a greater sin than breach of the ninth commandment but there is none more loathsome. It is a sudden intuition that Claggart is bearing false witness which goads Vere into the intemperate threat of the yard-arm-end, and so gives the master-at-arms his right to a full hearing; it is "horror" of his accuser, as against mere "amazement" at the accusation, that paralyzes Billy in Claggart's presence.

Can Melville's intention be doubted: to show Vere and Billy as bound to one another in a complementary greatness of soul? As the story moves on to the music of its close we are shown how each in his own way has instructed the other; how, so to speak, the magnanimity possible to virtuous innocence has fulfilled itself and in turn given its mysterious blessing to the world-sustaining magnanimity of experienced and commissioned virtue. The first represents that part of man which, being born to nature, remains of nature; the second represents that part of man which is uniquely of his own making, his defining burden as a moral and historical creature. Melville is explicit about what has happened. The "tension of agony" in Billy, he wrote, "survived not the something healing in the closeted interview with Captain Vere"; in turn Billy, restored to the role of "peacemaker," has lifted Vere, for all his anguish, beyond remorse. The motions of magnanimity under the most agonizing worldly duress: that is Melville's image and his theme.

By way of elaboration, we have been shown three fulfillments of
human nature—on one side depravity (or "monomania," his word for
Claggart as for Ahab), on the other these two forms of magnanimity self-
realized through recognition of one another. No exact balance is struck.
We sense some division of intention or disequilibrium. Midway in the
story, for example, it is the conflict between the two sides that engrosses
interest, or the attack of the one upon the other. But in the showdown
Claggart is not allowed to be any real match for the other two, and we
see that Melville's most profound intention lies further along. It is
seldom observed how pitiable Claggart is, in a way in which Billy and
Vere are not. Once acting in the open he cannot really deceive the Captain or leave any lasting scar on Billy—though his own understrappers
deceive him at will (chap. 14), as indeed he deceives himself; it is not
usually pointed out that Claggart believes his absurd accusation. He is
envious and despairing, an embodiment of those life-denying "sins
refined" which in *Clarel* were Melville's vision of Sodom and Gomorrah.
But he is not a hypocrite (as was Bland, the master-at-arms of *White-
Jacket*). In such a nature, Melville made a point of explaining, conscience functions not in restraint of its terrible determinations but as
their helpless agent. Also it is not usually observed how abruptly and entirely Claggart and what is embodied in him are dismissed from the
story. After the trial he is barely mentioned again; no trace of his con-
certed malignity is allowed to survive the interview between Vere and
Billy. It is as though Melville's conception of the radically opposing
crystallizations possible to human nature—confidence and envy, love
and hate, frankness and dissimulation, assurance and despair,
magnanimity and depravity—had swung clear of his tormenting search
for belief, so that he was free to rise at the climax of his story to a different and surer theme: the conjunction of the two magnanimities, making sacrifice to the military necessity.

IV

"The only great ones among mankind are the poet, the priest, and
the soldier; the man who sings, the man who blesses, and the man who
sacrifices, and sacrifices himself." It is not, I think, the grand design of
Christian myth nor the example of Greek tragedy or Miltonic epic but
this confessional aphorism of Baudelaire's that stands nearest the logic
and authority of *Billy Budd*. Strong judgments of life-in-general, of good
and evil and law and justice, may throb through Melville's narrative,

but its work is not to prove them. It asks not, "what is life?" or "what are the ways of God?" or even "what is justice?" but, "given this imaginable event in these circumstances, what power of response is there in certain phenomenal men?" So we are shown one kind of greatness of spirit in Vere, the soldier-priest of the military necessity, joining with another kind in Billy Budd, whose power to bless transfigures not only his own life. We observe, as in Baudelaire's journal or Vigny's *Servitudes et Grandeurs Militaires*, how an apprehension of the moral chaos and inscrutability of the experienced world has been held in balance by an austere intuition of honor and of personal abnegation. Yet for all their poignancy the specific terms of Melville's narrative do not require our option. Far less than in *Moby-Dick* or *Pierre* or *The Confidence-Man* or even *White-Jacket* are we asked to subscribe to some worldview. This is only a story, a narrative of "what befell" certain men in the year of the Great Mutiny. What does require our option, however, is the manner of the telling, the compassion and patiently exact utterance of the writer who has "sung" the story; for it is through these that we are brought to "believe" in the degree of virtue claimed for its protagonists.

"What one notices in him," E. M. Forster said of the Melville of *Billy Budd*, "is that his apprehensions are free from personal worry." His imagination and compassion work immediately, taking fair and full measure of their impressive objects. This cannot be said of all of Melville's work, in much of which (most damagingly in *Pierre*) all we can clearly see at times are the features of his own discomposure. And given the circumstances of the writing of *Billy Budd*—his career as an author of books thirty years behind him, his life closing down, his own two boys dead and his old energies gone—we might reasonably expect incoherence, failure of control. Instead we find a concentration, and integrity, of performance that match the best in his earlier career. The achievement, and the act of mind it speaks for, are indeed extraordinary. The particulars of this story positively invited misconstruction, as they still invite misinterpretation. Straining after dramatic effect of insistence on an allegorical lesson could only have diminished its authority. Mere indignation or pity would have left it no more than a parable of injustice, an exercise in resentment. But there is no indignation or outrage in the telling of *Billy Budd*—no quarrel at all, with God or society or law or nature or any agency of human suffering. Rather there is a poise and sureness of judgment (but at no loss of the appetite for explanation); a compassionate objectivity which, claiming no credit for itself, keeps its fine temper before the worst appearances; most of all, a readiness of apprehension possible only to an actual, measurable greatness of mind. That is to say, there is intellectual magnanimity — which Milton proposed in his treatise on Christian doctrine as the greatest of that "first class of special virtues connected with the duty of man towards himself."

This is the example the Melville of *Billy Budd* offers as a writer. A personal example, of course, but also a formal example, and of the most radical sort — as Henry James would remind us in declaring that "the deepest quality of a work of art will always be the quality of the mind of the producer." If we add that this quality does not come full-blown into the world but must be made and exercised, like any rational creation, then we may at least imagine how Melville's still barely tapped capacity to "influence" might yet be productively exploited, and his legacy as a writer husbanded and renewed.

Melville's Fist: The Execution of *Billy Budd*

Barbara Johnson

THE SENSE OF AN ENDING

Truth uncompromisingly told will always have its ragged edges; hence the conclusion of such a narration is apt to be less finished than an architectural finial.

MELVILLE, *Billy Budd*

The plot of Melville's *Billy Budd* is well known, and, like its title character, appears entirely straightforward and simple. It is a tale of three men in a boat: the innocent, ignorant foretopman, handsome Billy Budd; the devious, urbane master-at-arms, John Claggart; and the respectable, bookish commanding officer, Captain the Honorable Edward Fairfax ("Starry") Vere. Falsely accused by Claggart of plotting mutiny aboard the British man-of-war *Bellipotent*, Billy Budd, his speech impeded by a stutter, strikes his accuser dead in front of the captain, and is condemned, after a summary trial, to hang.

In spite of the apparent straightforwardness of the facts of the case, however, there exists in the critical literature on *Billy Budd* a notable range of disagreement over the ultimate meaning of the tale. For some, the story constitutes Melville's "testament of acceptance," his "everlasting yea," his "acceptance of tragedy," or at least his "recognition of necessity." For others, Melville's "final stage" is, on the contrary,

From *Studies in Romanticism* 18, no. 4 (Winter 1979).© 1979 by the Trustees of Boston University.

"irony": *Billy Budd* is considered a "testament of resistance," "ironic social criticism," or the last vituperation in Melville's "quarrel with God." More recently, critical attention has devoted itself to the ambiguity in the story, sometimes deploring it, sometimes revelling in it, and sometimes simply listing it. The ambiguity is attributed to various causes: the unfinished state of the manuscript, Melville's change of heart toward Vere, Melville's unreconciled ambivalence toward authority or his guilt about paternity, the incompatibility between the "plot" and the "story." But however great the disagreement over the meaning of this posthumous novel, all critics seem to agree in considering it Melville's "last word." "With the mere fact of the long silence in our minds," writes John Middleton Murry, "we could not help regarding 'Billy Budd' as the last will and spiritual testament of a man of genius."

To regard a story as its author's last will and testament is clearly to grant it a privileged, determining position in the body of that author's work. As its name implies, the "will" is taken to represent the author's final "intentions": in writing his will, the author is presumed to have summed up and evaluated his entire literary output, and directed it — as proof against "dissemination" — toward some determinable destination. The "ending" thus somehow acquires the metalinguistic authority to confer finality and intelligibility upon all that precedes it.

Now, since this sense of Melville's ending is so central to *Billy Budd* criticism, it might be useful to take a look at the nature of the ending of the story itself. Curiously enough, we find that *Billy Budd* ends not once, but no less than four times. As Melville himself describes it, the story continues far beyond its "proper" end: "How it fared with the Handsome Sailor during the year of the Great Mutiny has been faithfully given. But though *properly* the story ends with his life, something in the way of sequel will not be amiss" [*Billy Budd*, in *Billy Budd, Sailor and Other Stories*, ed. Harold Beaver (New York: Penguin Books, 1967), p. 405; unless otherwise indicated, all references to *Billy Budd* are to this edition] (emphasis mine here and passim). This "sequel" consists of "three brief chapters": (1) the story of the death of Captain Vere after an encounter with the French ship, the *Athée*; (2) a transcription of the Budd-Claggart affair published in an "authorized" naval publication, in which the characters of the two men are reversed, with Budd represented as the depraved villain and Claggart as the heroic victim; and (3) a description of the posthumous mythification of Billy Budd by his fellow sailors and a transcription of the ballad written by one of them, which presents itself as a monologue spoken by Billy on the eve of his execution. Billy Budd's last words, like Melville's own, are thus spoken posthumously — indeed the final line of the story is uttered from the bottom of the sea.

The question of the sense of Melville's ending is thus raised *in* the story as well as *by* the story. But far from tying up the loose ends of a confusing literary life, Melville's last words are an affirmation of the necessity of "ragged edges":

> The symmetry of form attainable in pure fiction cannot so readily be achieved in a narration essentially having less to do with fable than with fact. Truth uncompromisingly told will always have its ragged edges; hence the conclusion of such a narration is apt to be less finished than an architectural finial (p. 405).

The story ends by fearlessly fraying its own symmetry, thrice transgressing its own "proper" end; there is something inherently improper about this testamentary disposition of Melville's literary property. Indeed, far from totalizing itself into intentional finality, the story in fact begins to repeat itself — retelling itself first in reverse, and then in verse. The ending not only lacks special authority, it problematizes the very *idea* of authority by placing its own reversal in the pages of an "authorized" naval chronicle. To end is to repeat, and to repeat is to be ungovernably open to revision, displacement, and reversal. The sense of Melville's ending is to empty the ending of any privileged control over sense.

THE PLOT AGAINST THE CHARACTERS

For Tragedy is an imitation, not of men, but of action and of life, and life consists in action, and its end is a mode of action, not a quality. Now character determines men's qualities, but it is by their actions that they are happy or the reverse.
ARISTOTLE, *Poetics*

In beginning our study of *Billy Budd* with its ending, we, too, seem to have reversed the "proper" order of things. Most studies of the story tend to begin, after a few general remarks about the nature of good and evil, with a delineation of the three main characters: Billy, Claggart, and Vere. As Charles Weir puts it, "The purely physical action of the story is clear enough, and about its significant details there is never any doubt. . . . It is, therefore, with some consideration of the characters of the three principal actors that any analysis must begin." "Structurally," writes F. B. Freeman, "the three characters *are* the novel" (emphasis in original).

Melville goes to great lengths to describe both the physical and the moral characteristics of his protagonists. Billy Budd, a twenty-one-year-old "novice in the complexities of factitious life," is remarkable for his "significant personal beauty," "reposeful good nature," "straight-forward simplicity" and "unconventional rectitude." But Billy's intelligence ("such as it was," says Melville) is as primitive as his virtues are pristine. He is illiterate, he cannot understand ambiguity, and he stutters.

Claggart, on the other hand, is presented as the very image of urbane, intellectualized, articulate evil. Although "of no ill figure upon the whole" (p. 342), something in Claggart's pallid face consistently inspires uneasiness and mistrust. He is a man, writes Melville, "in whom was the mania of an evil nature, not engendered by vicious training or corrupting books or licentious living, but born with him and innate, in short, 'a depravity according to nature'" (p. 354). The mere sight of Billy Budd's rosy beauty and rollicking innocence does not fail to provoke in such a character "an antipathy spontaneous and profound" (p. 351).

The third man in the drama, who has inspired the greatest critical dissent, is presented in less vivid but curiously more contradictory terms. The *Bellipotent's* captain is described as both unaffected and pedantic, dreamy and resolute, irascible and undemonstrative, "mindful of the welfare of his men, but never tolerating an infraction of discipline," "intrepid to the verge of temerity, though never injudiciously so" (p. 338). While Billy and Claggart are said to owe their characters to "nature," Captain Vere is shaped mainly by his fondness for books:

> He loved books, never going to sea without a newly replenished library, compact but of the best. . . . With nothing of that literary taste which less heeds the thing conveyed than the vehicle, his bias was toward those books to which every serious mind of superior order occupying any active post of authority in the world naturally inclines: books treating of actual men and events no matter of what era — history, biography, and unconventional writers like Montaigne, who, free from cant and convention, honestly and in the spirit of common sense philosophize upon realities (p. 340).

Vere, then, is an honest, serious reader, seemingly well suited for the role of judge and witness that in the course of the story he will come to play.

No consideration of the nature of character in *Billy Budd*, however, can fail to take into account the fact that the fate of each of the characters is the direct reverse of what one is led to expect from his "nature." Billy is sweet, innocent, and harmless, yet he kills. Claggart is evil, perverted, and mendacious, yet he dies a victim. Vere is sagacious and responsible, yet he allows a man whom he feels to be blameless to hang. It is this discrepancy between character and action that gives rise to the critical disagreement over the story: readers tend either to save the plot and condemn Billy ("acceptance," "tragedy," or "necessity"), or to save Billy and condemn the plot ("irony," "injustice," or "social criticism").

In an effort to make sense of this troubling incompatibility between character and plot, many readers are tempted to say of Billy and Claggart, as does William York Tindall, that "each is more important for what he is than what he does. . . . Good and bad, they occupy the region of good and evil." This reading effectively preserves the allegorical values suggested by Melville's opening chapters, but it does so only by denying the importance of the plot. It ends where the plot begins: with the identification of the moral natures of the characters. One may therefore ask whether the allegorical interpretation (good vs. evil) depends as such on this sort of preference for being over doing, and if so, what effect the incompatibility between character and action may have on the allegorical functioning of *Billy Budd*.

Interestingly enough, Melville both invites an allegorical reading and subverts the very terms of its consistency when he writes of the murder: "Innocence and guilt personified in Claggart and Budd in effect changed places" (p. 380). Allowing for the existence of personification but reversing the relation between the personifier and personified, positioning an opposition between good and evil only to make each term take on the properties of its opposite, Melville sets up his plot in the form of a chiasmus:

This story, which is often read as a retelling of the story of Christ, is thus literally a cruci-fiction — a fiction structured in the shape of a cross. At the moment of the reversal, an instant before his fist shoots out, Billy's face seems to mark out the point of crossing, bearing "an expression which was as a crucifixion to behold" (p. 376). Innocence and guilt, criminal and victim, change places through the mute expressiveness of Billy's inability to speak.

If *Billy Budd* is indeed an allegory, it is an allegory of the questioning of the traditional conditions of allegorical stability. The requirement of Melville's plot that the good act out the evil designs of the bad while the bad suffer the unwarranted fate of the good indicates that the real opposition with which Melville is preoccupied here is less the static opposition between evil and good than the dynamic opposition between a man's "nature" and his acts, or, in Tindall's terms, the relation between human "being" and human "doing."

Curiously enough, it is precisely this question of being versus doing that is brought up by the only sentence we ever see Claggart directly address to Billy Budd. When Billy accidentally spills his soup across the path of the master-at-arms, Claggart playfully replies, "Handsomely done, my lad! And handsome *is* as handsome *did* it, too!" (p. 350). The proverbial expression "handsome is as handsome does," from which this exclamation springs, posits the possibility of a continuous, predictable, transparent relationship between being and doing. It supposes that the inner goodness of Billy Budd is in harmonious accord with his fair appearance, that, as Melville writes of the stereotypical "Handsome Sailor" in the opening pages of the story, "the moral nature" is not "out of keeping with the physical make" (p. 322). But it is this very continuity between the physical and the moral, between appearance and action, or between being and doing, that Claggart questions in Billy Budd. He warns Captain Vere not to be taken in by Billy's physical beauty: "You have but noted his fair cheek. A mantrap may be under the ruddy-tipped daisies" (p. 372). Claggart indeed soon finds his suspicions confirmed with a vengeance: when he repeats his accusation in front of Billy, the master-at-arms is struck down dead. It would thus seem that to question the continuity between character and action cannot be done with impunity, that fundamental questions of life and death are always surreptitiously involved.

In an effort to examine what is at stake in Claggart's accusation, it might be helpful to view the opposition between Billy and Claggart as an opposition not between innocence and guilt but between two conceptions of language, or between two types of reading. Billy seemingly represents the perfectly *motivated* sign; that is, his inner self (the signified) is considered transparently readable from the beauty of his outer self (the signifier). His "straightforward simplicity" is the very opposite of the "moral obliquities" or "crookedness of heart" that characterize "citified" or rhetorically sophisticated man. "To deal in double meanings and insinuations of any sort," writes Melville, "was quite foreign to his nature" (p. 327). In accordance with his "nature," Billy reads everything at face value, never questioning the meaning of appearances. He is dumbfounded at the Dansker's suggestion, "incomprehensible to a novice," that Claggart's very pleasantness can be interpreted as its opposite, as a sign that he is "down on" Billy Budd. To Billy, "the occasional frank air and pleasant word *went for what they purported to be*, the young sailor never having heard as yet of the 'too fair-spoken man' " (pp. 365-66). As a reader, then, Billy is symbolically as well as factually illiterate. His literal-mindedness is represented by his illiteracy because, in assuming that language can be taken at face value, he excludes the very functioning of *difference* that makes the act of reading both indispensable and undecidable.

Claggart, on the other hand, is the image of difference and duplicity, both in his appearance and in his character. His face is not ugly, but it hints of something defective or abnormal. He has no vices, yet he incarnates evil. He is an intellectual, but uses reason as "an ambidexter implement for effecting the irrational" (p. 354). Billy inspires in him both "profound antipathy" and "soft yearning." In the incompatibility of his attributes, Claggart is thus a personification of ambiguity and ambivalence, of the distance between signifier and signified, of the separation between being and doing: "apprehending the good, but powerless to be it, a nature like Claggart's . . . what recourse is left to it but to recoil upon itself" (p. 356). As a reader, Claggart has learned to "exercise a distrust keen in proportion to the fairness of the appearance" (p. 364). He is properly an ironic reader, who, assuming the sign to be arbitrary and unmotivated, reverses the value signs of appearances and takes a daisy for a mantrap and an unmotivated accidental spilling of soup for an intentional, sly escape of antipathy. Claggart meets his downfall, however, when he attempts to master the arbitrariness of the sign for his own ends by falsely (that is, arbitrarily) accusing Billy of harboring arbitrariness, of hiding a mutineer beneath the appearance of a baby.

Such a formulation of the Budd/Claggart relationship enables one to take a new look not only at the story itself but at the criticism as well. For this opposition between the literal reader (Billy) and the ironic reader (Claggart) is reenacted in the critical readings of *Billy Budd* in the opposition between the "acceptance" school and the "irony" school. Those who see the story as a "testament of acceptance" tend to take Billy's final benediction of Vere at face value; as Lewis Mumford puts it, "As Melville's own end approached, he cried out with Billy Budd: God Bless Captain Vere! In this final affirmation Herman Melville died." In contrast, those who read the tale ironically tend to take Billy's sweet fare-well as Melville's bitter curse. Joseph Schiffman writes, "At heart a kind man, Vere, strange to say, makes possible the depraved Claggart's wish — the destruction of Billy. 'God bless Captain Vere!' Is this not pierc-ing irony? As innocent Billy utters these words, does not the reader gag?" But since the acceptance/irony dichotomy is already contained within the story, since it is obviously one of the things the story is *about*, it is not enough to try to decide which of the readings is correct. What the reader of *Billy Budd* must do is to analyze what is at stake in the very opposition bet-ween literality and irony. This question, crucial for an understanding of *Billy Budd* not only as a literary but also as a critical phenomenon, will be taken up again in the final pages of [this essay], but first let us examine fur-ther the linguistic implications of the murder itself.

The Fiend That Lies Like Truth

Outwardly regarded, our craft is a lie; for all that is outwardly seen of it is the clean-swept deck, and oft-painted planks comprised above the water-line; whereas, the vast mass of our fabric, with all its store-rooms of secrets, forever slides along far under the surface.

Melville, White-Jacket

If Claggart's accusation that Billy is secretly plotting mutiny is essen-tially an affirmation of the possibility of a discontinuity between being and doing, of an arbitrary; nonmotivated relation between signifier and signified, then Billy's blow must be read as an attempt violently to deny that discontinuity or arbitrariness. The blow, as a denial, functions as a substitute for speech, as Billy explains during his trial: "I did not mean to kill him. Could I have used my tongue I would not have struck him. But he foully lied to my face and in presence of my captain, and I had to say something, and I could only say it with a blow" (p. 383). But in striking a blow in defense of the sign's motivation, Billy actually personifies the very *absence* of motivation: "I did not mean. . ." His blow is involuntary, ac-cidental, properly unmotivated. He is a sign that does not mean to mean. Billy, who cannot understand ambiguity, who takes pleasant words at face value and then obliterates Claggart for suggesting that one could do otherwise, whose sudden blow is a violent denial of any discrepancy bet-ween his being and his doing, ends up radically illustrating the very discrepancy he denies.

The story thus takes place between the postulate of continuity between signifier and signified ("handsome is as handsome does") and the postulate of their discontinuity ("a mantrap may be under the ruddy-tipped daisies"). Claggart, whose accusations of incipient mutiny are apparently false and therefore illustrate the very double-facedness that they attribute to Billy, is negated for proclaiming the lie about Billy which Billy's act of negation paradoxically proves to be the truth.

This paradox can also be stated in another way, in terms of the opposition between the performative and the constative functions of language. Constative language is language used as an instrument of cognition — it describes, reports, speaks *about* something other than itself. Performative language is language that itself functions as an act, not as a report of one. Promising, betting, swearing, marrying, and declaring war, for example, are not descriptions of acts but acts in their own right. The proverb "handsome is as handsome does" can thus also be read as a statement of the compatibility between the constative (being) and the performative (doing) dimensions of language. But what Billy's act dramatizes is their radical *incompatibility* — Billy performs the truth of Claggart's report to Vere only by means of his absolute and blind denial of its cognitive validity. If Billy had understood the truth, he would not have performed it. Handsome cannot both be and do its own undoing. The knowledge that being and doing are incompatible cannot know the ultimate performance of its own confirmation.

Melville's chiasmus thus creates a reversal not only of the places of guilt and innocence but also of the postulate of continuity and the postulate of discontinuity between doing and being, performance and cognition. When Billy's fist strikes Claggart's forehead, it is no longer possible for knowing and doing to meet. Melville's story does not report the occurence of a particularly deadly performative utterance, the tale itself performs the radical incompatibility between knowledge and acts.

All this, we recall, is triggered by a stutter, a linguistic defect. No analysis of the story's dramatization of linguistic categories can be complete without careful attention to this glaring infelicity. Billy's "vocal defect" is presented and explained in the story in the following terms:

> There was just one thing amiss in him . . . an occasional liability to a vocal defect. Though in the hour of elemental uproar or peril he was everything that a sailor should be, yet under sudden provocation of strong heart-feeling his voice, otherwise singularly musical, as if expressive of the harmony

within, was apt to develop an organic hesitancy, in fact more or less of a stutter or even worse. In this particular Billy was a striking instance that the arch interferer, the envious marplot of Eden, still has more or less to do with every human consignment to this planet of Earth. In every case, one way or another he is sure to slip in his little card, as much as to remind us — I too have a hand here (pp. 331-32).

It is doubtless this satanic "hand" that shoots out when Billy's speech fails him. Billy is all too literally a "*striking* instance" of the workings of the "envious marplot."

Melville's choice of the word *marplot* to characterize the originator of Billy's stutter deserves special note. It seems logical to understand that the stutter "mars" the plot in that it triggers the reversal of roles between Billy and Claggart. Yet in another sense this reversal does not mar the plot, it constitutes it. Here, as in the story of Eden, what the envious marplot mars is not the plot, but the state of plotlessness that exists "in the beginning." What both the Book of Genesis and *Billy Budd* narrate is thus not the story of a fall, but a fall into story.

In this connection, it is relevant to recall that Claggart falsely accuses Billy of instigating a *plot*, of stirring up mutiny against the naval authorities. What Claggart is in a sense doing by positing this fictitious plot is trying desperately to scare up a plot for the story. And it is Billy's very act of denial of his involvement in any plot that finally brings him *into* the plot. Billy's involuntary blow is an act of mutiny not only against the authority of his naval superiors but also against the authority of his own conscious intentions. Perhaps it is not by chance that the word *plot* can mean both "intrigue" and "story." If all plots somehow tell the story of their own marring, then perhaps it could be said that all plots are plots against authority, that authority creates the scene of its own destruction, that all stories necessarily recount by their very existence the subversion of the father, of the gods, of consciousness, of order, of expectations, or of meaning.

But is Billy truly as "plotless" as he appears? Does his "simplicity" hide no division, no ambiguity? As many critics have remarked, Billy's character seems to result mainly from his exclusion of the negative. When informed that he is being arbitrarily impressed for service on a man-of-war, Billy "makes no demur" (p. 323). When invited to a clandestine meeting by a mysterious stranger, Billy acquiesces through his "incapacity of plumply saying *no*" (p. 359, emphasis in original). But it is interesting to note that although Billy thus seems to be "just a boy who cain't say no," almost all the words used to describe him are negative in form: innocent, unconventional, illiterate, unsophisticated, unadulterate, etc. And although he denies any discrepency between what is said and what is meant, he does not prove to be totally incapable of lying. When asked about the shady visit of the afterguardsman, he distorts his account in order to edit out anything that indicates any incompatibility with the absolute maintenance of authority. He neglects to report the questionable proposition even though "it was his duty as a loyal blue-jacket" (p. 362) to do so. In thus shrinking from "the dirty work of a tell-tale" (p. 362), Billy maintains his "plotlessness" not spontaneously but through a complex act of filtering. Far from being simply and naturally pure, he is obsessed with maintaining his own irreproachability in the eyes of authority. After witnessing a flogging, he is so horrified that he resolves "that never through remissness would he make himself liable to such a visitation or do or omit aught that might merit even verbal reproof" (p. 346). Billy does not simply exclude the negative; he re-presses it. His reaction to questionable behavior of any sort (such as that of Red Whiskers, the afterguardsman, Claggart) is to obliterate it. He retains his "*blank* ignorance" (p. 363) only by a vigorous act of erasing. As Melville says of Billy's reaction to Claggart's petty provocations, "the ineffectual speculations into which he was led were so disturbingly alien to him that *he did his best to smother them*" (p. 362).

> In his *disgustful recoil* from an overture which, though he but ill comprehended, he *instinctively knew* must involve evil of some sort, Billy Budd was like a young horse fresh from the pasture suddenly inhaling a vile whiff from some chemical factory, and by repeated snortings trying to *get it out* of his nostrils and lungs. This frame of mind *barred all desire* of holding further parley with the fellow, even were it but for the purpose of gaining some enlightenment as to his design in approaching him (p. 361).

Billy maintains his purity only through constant, though unconscious, censorship. "Innocence," writes Melville, "was his blinder" (p. 366).

It is interesting to note that while the majority of readers see Billy as a personification of goodness and Claggart as a personification of evil, those who do not, tend to read from a psychoanalytical point of view. Much has been made of Claggart's latent homosexuality, which Melville clearly suggests. Claggart, like the hypothetical "X —," "is a nut not to be cracked by the tap of a lady's fan" (p. 352). The "unobserved glance" he sometimes casts upon Billy contains "a touch of soft yearning, as if Claggart could even have loved Billy but for fate and ban" (p. 365). The spilling of the soup and Claggart's reaction to it are often read symbolically as a sexual exchange, the import of which, of course, is lost on Billy, who cannot read.

According to this perspective, Claggart's so-called evil is thus really a repressed form of love. But it is perhaps even more interesting to examine the way in which the psychoanalytical view treats Billy's so-called goodness as being in reality a repressed form of hate:

> The persistent feminine imagery . . . indicate[s] that Billy has identified himself with the mother at a pre-Oedipean level and has adopted the attitude of harmlessness and placation toward the father in order to avoid the hard struggle of the Oedipus conflict. . . . That all Billy's rage and hostility against the father are unconscious is symbolized by the fact that whenever aroused it cannot find expression in spoken language. . . . This is a mechanism for keeping himself from admitting his own guilt and his own destructiveness.

> All of Billy's conscious acts are toward passivity. . . . In symbolic language, Billy Budd is seeking his own castration — seeking to yield up his vitality to an authoritative but kindly father, whom he finds in Captain Vere.

> Quite often a patient begins to stutter when he is particularly eager to prove a point. Behind his apparent zeal he has concealed a hostile or sadistic tendency to destroy his opponent by means of words, and the stuttering is both a blocking of and a punishment for this tendency. Still more often stuttering is exacerbated by the presence of prominent or authoritative persons, that is, of paternal figures against whom the unconscious hostility is most intense.

> Although *Billy Budd, Sailor* is placed in historical time . . . the warfare is not between nations for supremacy on the seas but between father and son in the eternal warfare to determine succession.

> When Vere becomes the father, Claggart and Billy are no

longer sailors but sons in rivalry for his favor and blessing. Claggart manifestly is charging mutiny but latently is accusing the younger son or brother of plotting the father's overthrow. . . . When Billy strikes Claggart with a furious blow to the forehead, he puts out the "evil eye" of his enemy-rival, but at the same time the blow is displaced, since Billy is prohibited from striking the father. After Claggart is struck and lies on the deck "a dead snake," Vere covers his face in silent recognition of the displaced blow.

Billy's type of innocence is . . . *pseudoinnocence.* . . . Capitalizing on naiveté, it consists of a childhood that is never outgrown, a kind of fixation on the past. . . . When we face questions too big and too horrendous to contemplate . . . we tend to shrink into this kind of innocence and make a virtue of powerlessness, weakness, and helplessness. . . . It is this innocence that cannot come to terms with the destructiveness in one's self or others; and hence, as with Billy Budd, it actually becomes self-destructive.

The psychoanalytical reading is thus a demystification of the notion of innocence portrayed in *Billy Budd.* In the psychoanalytical view, what underlies the metaphysical lament that in this world "goodness is impotent" is the idea that impotence is good, that harmlessness is innocent, that naiveté is lovable, that "giving no cause of offense to anybody" and resolving never "to do or omit aught that might merit . . . reproof" (p. 346) are the highest ideals in human conduct. While most readers react to Billy as do his fellow crew-members ("they all love him," [p. 325]), the psychoanalysts share Claggart's distrust ("for all his youth and good looks, a deep one," [p. 371]) and even disdain ("to be nothing more than innocent!" [p. 356]).

In this connection it is curious to note that while the psychoanalysts have implicitly chosen to adopt the attitude of Claggart, Melville, in the crucial confrontation scene, comes close to presenting Claggart as a psychoanalyst:

With the measured step and calm collected air of an asylum physician approaching in the public hall some patient beginning to show indications of a coming paroxysm, Claggart deliberately advanced within short range of Billy, and, mesmerically looking him in the eye, briefly recapitulated the accusation (p. 375).

It is as though Claggart as analyst, in attempting to bring Billy's unconscious hostility to consciousness, unintentionally unleashes the destructive acting-out of transferential rage. The fatal blow, far from being an unmotivated accident, is the gigantic return of the power of negation that Billy has been repressing all his life. And in his blind destructiveness, Billy lashes out against the "father" as well as against the very process of analysis itself.

The difference between the psychoanalytical and the traditional "metaphysical" readings of *Billy Budd* lies mainly in the status accorded to the fatal blow. If Billy represents pure goodness, then his act is unintentional but symbolically righteous, since it results in the destruction of the "evil" Claggart. If Billy is a case of neurotic repression, then his act is determined by his unconscious desires, and reveals the destructiveness of the attempt to repress one's own destructiveness. In the first case, the murder is accidental; in the second, it is the fulfillment of a wish. Strangely enough, this question of accident versus motivation is brought up again at the end of the story, in the curious lack of spontaneous ejaculation in Billy's corpse. Whether the lack of spasm is as mechanical as its presence would have been, or whether it results from what the purser calls "will power" or "euthanasia," the incident stands as a negative analogue of the murder scene. In the former, it is the absence; in the later, the presence, of physical violence that offers a challenge to interpretation. The burlesque discussion of the "prodigy of repose" by the purser and the surgeon, interrupting as it does the solemnity of Billy's "ascension," can have no other purpose than to dramatize the central importance for the story of the question of arbitrary accident versus determinable motivation. If the psychoanalytical and the metaphysical readings, however incompatible, are both equally supported by textual evidence, then perhaps Melville, rather than asking us to choose between them, is presenting us with a context in which to examine what is at stake in the very oppositions between psychoanalysis and metaphysics, chance and determination, the willed and the accidental, the unconscious and the moral.

THE DEADLY SPACE BETWEEN

And thus do we of wisdom and of reach,
With windlasses and with assays of bias,
By indirections find directions out.
                                    Hamlet 2.1

While Billy stands as a performative riddle (are his actions motivated or accidental?), John Claggart is presented as an enigma for cognition, a man "who for reasons of his own was keeping *incog*" (p. 343).
Repeatedly referred to as a "mystery," Claggart, it seems, is difficult,
even perilous, to describe:

> For the adequate comprehending of Claggart by a normal na-
> ture these hints are insufficient. To pass from a normal
> nature to him one must cross "the deadly space between."
> And this is best done by indirection (p. 352).

Between Claggart and a "normal nature" there exists a gaping cognitive
chasm. In a literal sense, this image of crossing a "deadly space" in order
to reach Claggart can almost be seen as an ironic prefiguration of the
murder. Billy does indeed "cross" the "space" between himself and
Claggart by means of a "deadly" blow. The phrase "space between"
recurs, in fact, just after the murder, to refer to the physical separation
between the dead Claggart and the condemned Billy:

> Aft, and on either side, was a small stateroom, the one now
> temporarily a jail and the other a dead-house, and a yet
> smaller compartment, leaving a *space between* expanding for-
> ward (p. 382).

It is by means of a deadly chiasmus that the spatial chasm is crossed.

But physical separation is obviously not the only kind of "deadly
space" involved here. The expression "deadly space between" refers primarily to a gap in cognition, a boundary beyond which ordinary understanding does not normally go. This sort of space, which stands as a
limit to comprehension, seems to be an inherent feature of the attempt to
describe John Claggart. From the very beginning, Melville admits, "His
portrait I essay, but shall never hit it" (p. 342). What Melville says he
will *not* do here is precisely what Billy Budd *does* do: hit John Claggart. It
would seem that speaking and killing are thus mutually exclusive; Billy
Budd kills because he cannot speak, while Melville, through the very act
of speaking, does not kill. Billy's fist crosses the "deadly space" directly;
Melville's crossing, "done by indirection," leaves its target intact.

This state of affairs, reassuring as it sounds on a moral level, is
rather unsettling, however, if one examines what it implies about Melville's writing. For how reliable can a description be if it does not hit its
object? What do we come to know of John Claggart if what we learn is
that his portrait is askew? If to describe perfectly, to refer adequately,

would be to "hit" the referent and thus annihilate it; if to know completely would be to obliterate the very object known; if the perfect fulfillment of the constative, referential function of language would consist in the total obliteration of the object of that function; then language can retain its "innocence" only by giving up its referential validity. Melville can avoid murder only by grounding his discourse in ineradicable error. If to cross a space by indirection — that is, by rhetorical displacement — is to escape deadliness, that crossing can succeed only on the condition of radically losing its way.

It can thus be said that the "deadly space" that runs through *Billy Budd* is located between cognition and performance, knowing and doing, error and murder. But even this formulation is insufficient if it is taken to imply that doing is deadly while speaking is not, or that directness is murderous while avoidance is innocent. Melville does not simply recommend the replacement of doing by speaking or of direct by indirect language. He continues to treat obliquity and deviation as evils, and speaks of digression as a "literary sin":

> In this matter of writing, resolve as one may to keep to the main road, some bypaths have an enticement not readily to be withstood. I am going to err into such a bypath. If the reader will keep me company I shall be glad. At the least, we can promise ourselves that pleasure which is wickedly said to be in sinning, for a literary sin the divergence will be (p. 334).

Directness and indirectness are equally suspect and equally innocent. Further complications of the moral status of rhetoric will be examined later in this [essay], but first let us pursue the notion of the "deadly space."

If the space at work in *Billy Budd* cannot be located simply and unequivocally between language and action or between directness and indirection, where is it located and how does it function? Why is it the space itself that is called "deadly"? And how, more particularly, does Melville go about *not* hitting John Claggart?

Melville takes up the question of Claggart's "nature" many times. Each time, the description is proffered as a necessary key to the understanding of the story. And yet, each time, what we learn about the master-at-arms is that we cannot learn anything:

> Nothing was known of his former life (p. 343).

About as much was really known to the *Bellipotent's* tars of the master-at-arms' career before entering the service as an astronomer knows about a comet's travels prior to its first observable appearance in the sky (p. 345).

What can more partake of the mysterious than an antipathy spontaneous and profound . . . ? (p. 351).

Dark sayings are these, some will say. But why? Is it because they somewhat savor of Holy Writ in its phrase "mystery of iniquity?" (p. 354).

And, after informing us that the crossing of the "deadly space" between Claggart and a "normal nature" is "best done by indirection," Melville's narrator takes himself at his word; he digresses into a long fictitious dialogue between himself as a youth and an older "honest scholar" concerning a mysterious Mr. "X —" whose "labyrinth" cannot be penetrated by "knowledge of the world," a dialogue so full of periphrases that the youthful participant himself "did not quite see" its "drift" (p. 353). The very phrase "the deadly space between" is, according to editors Hayford and Sealts, a quotation of unknown origin; the source of the expression used to designate what is not known is thus itself unknown. Even the seemingly satisfactory Platonic definiton of Claggart's evil—"Natural Depravity: a depravity according to nature"—is in fact, as F. B. Freeman points out, nothing but a tautology. Syntactically, the definition fulfills its function, but it is empty of any cognitive information. The place of explanation and definition is repeatedly filled, but its content is always lacking. The progress of Melville's description describes an infinite regress of knowledge. The "deadly space" is situated not between Claggart and his fellow men, but within Melville's very attempts to account for him.

It would seem that rather than simply separating language from action, the space in question is also at work within language itself. In the tautology of Claggart's evil, it marks an empty articulation between the expression and its definition. Other linguistic spaces abound. What, indeed, is Billy's fateful stutter, if not a deadly gap in his ability to speak? The space opened up by the stutter is the pivot on which the entire story turns. And the last words of the dying Captain Vere, which stand in the place of ultimate commentary upon the drama, are simply "Billy Budd, Billy Budd," the empty repetition of a name. At all the crucial moments in the drama — in the origin of evil, in the trigger of the act, in the final assessment — the language of *Billy Budd* stutters. At those moments, the constative or referential content is eclipsed; language conveys only its own empty, mechanical functioning. But these very gaps in understanding are what Melville is asking us to understand.

The cognitive spaces marked out by these eclipses of meaning are important not because they mark the limits of interpretation but because they function as its cause. The gaps in understanding are never directly perceived as such by the characters in the novel; those gaps are themselves taken as interpretable signs and triggers for interpretation. The lack of knowledge of Claggart's past, for example, is seen as a sign that he has something to hide:

> Nothing was known of his former life. . . . Among certain grizzled sea gossips of the gun decks and forecastle went a rumor perdue that the master-at-arms was a *chevalier* [emphasis in original] who had volunteered into the King's navy by way of compounding for some mysterious swindle whereof he had been arraigned at the King's Bench. *The fact that nobody could substantiate this report was, of course, nothing against its secret currency.* . . . Indeed a man of Claggart's accomplishments, without prior nautical experience entering the navy at mature life, as he did, and necessarily allotted at the start to the lowest grade in it; a man too who never made allusion to his previous life ashore; these were circumstances which *in the dearth of exact knowledge* as to his true antecedents opened to the invidious *a vague field for unfavorable surmise* (p. 343).

In other words, the absence of knowledge here leads to the propagation of tales. The absence of knowledge of Claggart's origins is not a simple, contingent, theoretically remediable lack of information; it is the very *origin* of his "evil nature." Interestingly, in Billy's case, an equal lack of knowledge leads some readers to see his origin as divine. Asked who his father is, Billy replies, "God knows." The divine and the satanic can thus be seen as metaphysical interpretations of discontinuities in knowledge. In *Billy Budd*, a stutter and a tautology serve to mark the spot from which evil springs.

Evil, then, is essentially the misreading of discontinuity through the attribution of meaning to a space or division in language. But the fact that stories of Claggart's evil arise out of a seemingly meaningless gap in knowledge is hardly a meaningless or innocent fact in itself, either in its cause or in its consequences. Claggart's function is that of a police-man "charged among other matters with the duty of preserving order on the populous lower gun decks" (p. 342). As Melville points out, "no man holding his office in a man-of-war can ever hope to be popular with the crew" (p. 345). The inevitable climate of resentment surrounding the master-at-arms might itself be sufficient to turn the hypothesis of depravity into a self-fulfilling prophecy. As Melville puts it, "The point of the present story *turn[s]* *on the hidden nature* of the master-at-arms" (p. 354). The entire plot of *Billy Budd* could conceivably be seen as a con-sequence not of what Claggart does but of what he does not say.

It is thus by means of the misreading of gaps in knowledge and of discontinuities in action that the plot of *Billy Budd* takes shape. But because Melville describes both the spaces and the readings they engen-der, his concentration on the vagaries of interpretive error open up within the text the possibility of substantiating quite a number of "inside narratives" different from the one with which we are explicitly pre-sented. What Melville's tale tells is the snowballing of tale-telling. It is possible, indeed, to retell the story from a point of view that fully justifies Claggart's suspicions, merely buy putting together a series of indications already available in the narrative.

1. As Billy is being taken from the merchant ship to the warship, he shouts in farewell, "And good-bye to you too, old *Rights-of-Man*" (em-phasis in original). Ratcliffe, who later recounts the incident to Claggart (as is shown by the latter's referring to it in making his accusation to Vere), interprets this as "a sly slur at impressment in general, and that of himself in especial" (p. 327). The first information Claggart is likely to have gleaned on Billy Budd has thus passed through the filter of the lieu-tenant's interpretation that the handsome recruit's apparent gaiety con-ceals resentment.

2. When Billy resolves, after seeing the flogging of another novice, "never to merit reproof," his "punctiliousness in duty" (p. 346) is laughed at by his topmates. Billy tries desperately to make his actions coincide with his desire for perfect irreproachability, but he nevertheless finds himself "getting into petty trouble" (p. 346). Billy's "unconcealed anxiety" is considered "comical" by his fellows (p. 347). It is thus Billy's obsessive concern with his own perfection that starts a second snowball rolling, since Claggart undertakes a subtle campaign of petty persecutions "to try the temper of the man" (p. 358). The instrument used by Claggart to set "little traps for the worriment of the foretopman" is a corporal called "Squeak," who, "having naturally enough concluded that his master

could have no love for the sailor, made it his business, faithful under-strapper that he was, to foment the ill blood by perverting to his chief certain innocent frolics of the good-natured foretopman, besides inventing for his mouth sundry contumelious epithets he claimed to have overheard him let fall" (p. 357). Again, Claggart perceives Billy only through the distortion of an unfavorable interpretation.

3. With this impression of Billy already in his mind, Claggart proceeds to take Billy's spilling of the soup across his path "not for the mere accident it assuredly was, but for the sly escape of a spontaneous feeling on Billy's part more or less answering to the antipathy on his own" (p. 356). If this is an overreading, it is important to note that the critical tendency to see sexual or religious symbolism in the soup scene operates on exactly the same assumption as that made by Claggart — what appears to be an accident is actually motivated and meaningful. Claggart's spontaneous interpretation, hidden behind his playful words ("Handsomely done"), is not only legitimate enough on its own terms, but receives unexpected confirmation in Billy's naive outburst: "There now, who say that Jemmy Legs is down on me?" This evidence of a preexisting context in which Claggart, referred to by his disrespectful nickname, has been discussed by Billy with others — apparently a number of others, although in fact it is only one person — provides all the support Claggart needs to substantiate his suspicions. And still, he is willing to try another test.

4. Claggart sends an afterguardsman to Billy at night with a proposition to join a mutinous conspiracy of impressed men. Although Billy rejects the invitation, he does not report it as loyalty demands. He is thus protecting the conspirators. Claggart's last test has been completed; Billy is a danger to the ship. In his function as chief of police, it is Claggart's duty to report the danger.

This "reversed" reading is no more — but certainly no less — legitimate than the ordinary "good versus evil" interpretation. But its very possibility — evoked not only by these behind-the-scenes hints and nuances but also by the "garbled" newspaper report — can be taken as a sign of the centrality of the question of reading posed not only *by* but also *in* the text of *Billy Budd*. Far from recounting an unequivocal "clash of opposites" the confrontation between Billy and Claggart is built by a series of minute gradations and subtle insinuations. The opposites that clash here are not two *characters* but two *readings*.

Three Readings of Reading

It is no doubt significant that the character around whom the greatest critical dissent has revolved is neither the good one nor the evil one but the one who is explicitly presented as a *reader*, Captain Vere. On some level, readers of *Billy Budd* have always testified to the fact that reading, as much as killing, is at the heart of Melville's story. But how is the act of reading being manifested? And what, precisely, are its relations with the deadliness of the spaces it attempts to comprehend?

As we have noted, critical readings of *Billy Budd* have generally divided themselves into two opposing groups, the "testament of acceptance" school on the one hand and the "testament of resistance" or "irony" school on the other. The first is characterized by its tendency to take at face value the narrator's professed admiration of Vere's sagacity and the final benediction of Vere uttered by Billy. The second group is characterized by its tendency to distance the reader's point of view from that of any of the characters, including the narrator, so that the injustice of Billy's execution becomes perceptible through a process of reversal of certain explicit pronouncements within the tale. This opposition between "acceptance" and "irony" quite strikingly mirrors, as we mentioned earlier, the opposition within the story between Billy's naiveté and Claggart's paranoia. We will therefore begin our analysis of Melville's study of the nature of reading with an examination of the way in which the act of reading is manifested in the confrontation between these two characters.

It seems evident that Billy's reading method consists of taking everything at face value, while Claggart's consists of seeing a mantrap under every daisy. Yet in practice, neither of these methods is rigorously upheld. The naive reader is not naive enough to forget to edit out information too troubling to report. The instability of the space between sign and referent, normally denied by the naive reader, is called upon as an instrument whenever that same instability threatens to disturb the content of meaning itself. Billy takes every sign as transparently readable as long as what he reads is consistent with transparent peace, order, and authority. When this is not so, his reading clouds accordingly. And Claggart, for whom every sign can be read as its opposite, neglects to doubt the transparency of any sign that tends to confirm his own doubts: "the master-at-arms *never suspected the veracity*" (p. 357) of Squeak's reports. The naive believer thus refuses to believe any evidence that subverts the transparency of his beliefs, while the ironic doubter forgets to suspect the reliability of anything confirming his own suspicions.

Naiveté and irony thus stand as symmetrical opposites blinded by their very incapacity to see anything but symmetry. Claggart, in his antipathy, "can really form no conception of an *unreciprocated* malice" (p. 358). And Billy, conscious of his own blamelessness, can see nothing but pleasant- ness in Claggart's pleasant words: "Had the foretopman been conscious of having done or said anything to provoke the ill-will of the official, it would have been different with him, and his sight might have been purg- ed if not sharpened. As it was, innocence was his blinder" (p. 366). Each character sees the other only through the mirror of his own reflection. Claggart, looking at Billy, mistakes his own twisted face for the face of an enemy, while Billy, recognizing in Claggart the negativity he smothers in himself, strikes out.

The naive and the ironic readers are thus equally destructive, both of themselves and of each other. It is significant that both Billy and Clag- gart should die. Both readings do violence to the plays of ambiguity and belief by forcing upon the text the applicability of a universal and absolute law. The one, obsessively intent on preserving peace and elim- inating equivocation, murders the text; the other, seeing nothing but universal war, becomes the spot on which aberrant premonitions of negativity become truth.

But what of the third reader in the drama, Captain Vere? What can be said of a reading whose task is precisely to read the *relation* between naiveté and paranoia, acceptance and irony, murder and error?

For many readers, the function of Captain Vere has been to provide "complexity" and "reality" in an otherwise "oversimplified" allegorical confrontation:

> Billy and Claggart, who represent almost pure good and pure evil, are too simple and too extreme to satisfy the demands of realism; for character demands admixture. Their all but alle- gorical blackness and whiteness, however, are functional in the service of Vere's problem, and Vere, goodness knows, is real enough.

> *Billy Budd* seems different from much of the later work, less "mysterious," even didactic. . . . Its issues seem somewhat simplified, and, though the opposition of Christly Billy and Satanic Claggart is surely diagrammatic, it appears almost melodramatic in its reduction of values. Only Captain Vere seems to give the story complexity, his deliberations acting like a balance wheel in a watch, preventing a rapid, obvious

resolution of the action. . . . It is Vere's decision, and the debatable rationale for it, which introduces the complexity of intimation, the ambiguity.

As the locus of complexity, Captain Vere then becomes the "balance wheel" not only in the clash between good and evil but also in the clash between "accepting" and "ironic" interpretations of the story. Critical opinion has pronounced the captain "vicious" and "virtuous," "self-mythifying" and "self-sacrificing," "capable" and "cowardly," "responsible" and "criminal," "moral" and "perverted," "intellectual" and "stupid," "moderate" and "authoritarian." But how does the same character provoke such diametrically opposed responses? Why is it the judge that is so passionately judged?

In order to analyze what is at stake in Melville's portrait of Vere, let us first examine the ways in which Vere's reading differs from those of Billy Budd and John Claggart:

1. While the naive/ironic dichotomy was based on a symmetry between *individuals*, Captain Vere's reading takes place within a social *structure*: the rigidly hierarchical structure of a British warship. While the naive reader (Billy) destroys the other in order to defend the self, and while the ironic reader (Claggart) destroys the self by projecting agression onto the other, the third reader (Vere) subordinates both self and other, and ultimately sacrifices both self and other, for the preservation of a political order.

2. The apparent purpose of both Billy's and Claggart's readings was to determine character; to preserve innocence or to prove guilt. Vere, on the other hand, subordinates character to action, being to doing. "A martial court," he tells his officers, "must needs in the present case confine its attention to the *blow's consequence*, which consequence justly is to be deemed not otherwise than as the *striker's deed*" (p. 384).

3. In the opposition between the metaphysical and psychoanalytical readings of Billy's deed, the deciding question was whether the blow should be considered accidental or (unconsciously) motivated. But in Vere's courtroom reading, both these alternatives are irrelevant: "Budd's intent or non-intent is nothing to the purpose" (p. 389). What matters is not the cause but the consequences of the blow.

4. The naive or literal reader takes language at face value and treats signs as *motivated*; the ironic reader assumes that the relation between sign and meaning can be *arbitrary* and that appearances are made to be reversed. For Vere, the functions and meanings of signs are neither

transparent nor reversible but fixed by socially determined *convention*. Vere's very character is determined not by a relation between his outward appearance and his inner being but by the "buttons" that signify his position in society. While both Billy and Claggart are said to owe their character to "nature," Vere sees his actions and being as meaningful only within the context of a contractual allegiance:

> Do these buttons that we wear attest that our allegiance is to Nature? No, to the King. Though the ocean, which is inviolate Nature primeval, though this be the element where we move and have our being as sailors, yet as the King's officers lies our duty in a sphere correspondingly natural? So little is that true, that in receiving our commissions we in the most important regards ceased to be natural free agents. When war is declared are we the commissioned fighters previously consulted? We fight at command. If our judgments approve the war, that is but coincidence (p. 387).

Judgment is thus for Vere a function neither of individual conscience nor of absolute justice but of "the rigor of martial law" (p. 387) operating *through* him.

5. While Billy and Claggart read spontaneously and directly, Vere's reading often makes use of precedent (historical facts, childhood memories), allusions (to the Bible, to various ancient and modern authors), and analogies (Billy is like Adam, Claggart is like Ananias). Just as both Billy and Claggart have no known past, they read without memory; just as their lives end with their reading, they read without foresight. Vere, on the other hand, interrogates both past and future for interpretative guidance.

6. While Budd and Claggart thus oppose each other directly, without regard for circumstance or consequence, Vere reads solely in function of the attending historical situation; the Nore and Spithead mutinies have created an atmosphere "critical to naval authority" (p. 380), and, since an engagement with the enemy fleet is possible at any moment, the *Bellipotent* cannot afford internal unrest.

The fundamental factor that underlies the opposition between the metaphysical Budd/Claggart conflict on the one hand and the reading of Captain Vere on the other can be summed up in a single word: history. While the naive and the ironic readers attempt to impose upon language the functioning of an absolute, timeless, universal law (the sign as either motivated or arbitrary), the question of *martial* law arises within the story precisely to reveal the law as a historical phenomenon, to underscore the element of contextual mutability in the conditions of any act of reading. Arbitrariness and motivation, irony and literality, are parameters between which language constantly fluctuates, but only historical context determines which proportion of each is perceptible to each reader. Melville indeed shows history to be a story not only of events but also of fluctuations in the very functioning of irony and belief:

> The event *converted into irony for a time* those spirited strains of Dibdin (p. 333).

> Everything is *for a term venerated* in navies (p. 408).

The opposing critical judgments of Vere's decision to hang Billy are divided, in the final analysis, according to the place they attribute to history in the process of justification. For the ironists, Vere is misusing history for his own self-preservation or for the preservation of a world safe for aristocracy. For those who accept Vere's verdict as tragic but necessary, it is Melville who has stacked the historical cards in Vere's favor. In both cases, the conception of history as interpretive instrument remains the same: it is its *use* that is being judged. And the very direction of *Billy Budd* criticism itself, historically moving from acceptance to irony, is no doubt itself interpretable in the same historical terms.

Evidence can be found in the text for both pro-Vere and anti-Vere judgments:

> Full of disquietude and misgiving, the surgeon left the cabin. Was Captain Vere suddenly affected in his mind? (p. 378).

> Whether Captain Vere, as the surgeon professionally and privately surmised, was really the sudden victim of any degree of aberration, every one must determine for himself by such light as this narrative may afford (pp. 379-80).

> That the unhappy event which has been narrated could not have happened at a worse juncture was but too true. For it was close on the heel of the suppressed insurrections, an after-time very critical to naval authority, demanding from every English sea commander two qualities not readily inter-fusable — prudence and rigor (p. 380).

> Small wonder then that the *Bellipotent's* captain . . . felt that cir-
> cumspection not less than promptitude was necessary. . . .
> Here he may or may not have erred (p. 380).

The effect of these explicit oscillations of judgment within the text is to
underline the importance of the act of judging while rendering its outcome undecidable. Judgment, however difficult, is clearly the central
preoccupation of Melville's text, whether it be the judgment pronounced
by Vere or *upon* him.

There is still another reason for the uncertainty over Vere's final
status, however: the unfinished state of the manuscript at Melville's
death. According to editors Hayford and Sealts, it is the "late pencil revi-
sions" that cast the greatest doubt upon Vere; Melville was evidently still
fine-tuning the text's attitude toward its third reader when he died. The
ultimate irony in the tale is thus that our final judgment of the very
reader who takes history into consideration is made problematic by the
intervention of history; by the historical accident of the author's death.
History here affects interpretation not only within the content of the narration but also within the very production of the narrative. And what remains suspended by this historical accident is nothing less than the exact
signifying value of history. Clearly, the meaning of "history" as a feature
distinguishing Vere's reading from those of Claggart and Budd can in no
way be taken for granted.

JUDGMENT AS POLITICAL PERFORMANCE

*When a poet takes his seat on the tripod of the Muse, he cannot control his
thoughts. . . . When he represents men with contrasting characters he is often obliged
to contradict himself, and he doesn't know which of the opposing speeches contains
the truth. But for the legislator, this is impossible: he must not let his laws say two
different things on the same subject.*

PLATO, *The Laws*

In the final analysis, the question is not, What did Melville really
think of Captain Vere? but rather, What is at stake in his way of presenting him? What can we learn from him about the act of judging? Melville
seems to be presenting us less with an object for judgment than with an
example of judgment. And the very vehemence with which the critics
tend to praise or condemn the justice of Vere's decision indicates that it
is judging, not murdering, that Melville is asking us to judge.

And yet Vere's judgment *is* an act of murder. Captain Vere is a reader who kills, not, like Billy, instead of speaking, but rather, precisely by means of speaking. While Billy kills through verbal impotence, Vere kills through the very potency and sophistication of rhetoric. Judging, in Vere's case, is nothing less than the wielding of the power of life and death through language. In thus occupying the point at which murder and language meet, Captain Vere positions himself astride the "deadly space between." While Billy's performative force occupies the vanishing point of utterance and cognition, and while the validity of Claggart's cognitive perception is realized only through the annihilation of the perceiver, Captain Vere's reading mobilizes both power and knowledge, performance and cognition, error and murder. Judgment is cognition functioning as an act. This combination of performance and cognition defines Vere's reading not merely as historical but as political. If politics is defined as the attempt to reconcile action with understanding, then Melville's story offers an exemplary context in which to analyze the interpretive and performative structures that make politics so problematic.

Melville's story amply demonstrates that the alliance between knowledge and action is by no means an easy one. Vere indeed has often been seen as the character in the tale who experiences the greatest suffering; his understanding of Billy's character and his military duty are totally at odds. On the one hand, cognitive exactitude requires that "history" be taken into consideration. Yet what constitutes "knowledge of history"? How are "circumstances" to be defined? What sort of causality does "precedent" imply? And what is to be done with overlapping but incompatible "contexts"? Before deciding upon innocence and guilt, Vere must define and limit the frame of reference within which his decision is to be possible. He does so by choosing the "legal" context over the "essential" context:

> In a *legal view* the apparent victim of the tragedy was he who had sought to victimize a man blameless; and the indisputable deed of the latter, *navally regarded*, constituted the most heinous of military crimes. Yet more. The *essential right and wrong* involved in the matter, the clearer that might be, so much the worse for the responsibility of a loyal sea commander, inasmuch as he was not authorized to determine the matter on that primitive basis (p. 380).

Yet it is precisely this determination of the proper frame of reference that dictates the outcome of the decision; once Vere has defined his context, he has also in fact reached his verdict. The very choice of the *conditions* of judgment itself constitutes a judgment. But what are the conditions of choosing the conditions of judgment?

The alternative, it seems, is between the "naval" and the "primitive," between "Nature" and "the King," between the martial court and what Vere calls the "Last Assizes" (p. 388). But the question arises of exactly what the concept "Nature" entails in such an opposition. In what way, and with what changes, would it have been possible for Vere's allegiance to be to "Nature"? How can a legal judgment exemplify "primitive" justice?

In spite of his allegiance to martial law and conventional authority, Vere clearly finds the "absolute" criteria equally applicable to Billy's deed, for he responds to each new development with the following exclamations:

> "It is the divine judgment on Ananias!" (p. 278).

> "Struck dead by an angel of God! Yet the angel must hang!" (p. 378).

> "Before a court less arbitrary and more merciful than a martial one, that plea would largely extenuate. At the Last Assizes it shall acquit" (p. 388).

> "Ay, there is a mystery; but, to use a scriptural phrase, it is a 'mystery of iniquity,' a matter for psychologic theologicans to discuss" (p. 385).

This last expression, which refers to the source of Claggart's antipathy, has already been mentioned by Melville's narrator and dismissed as being "tinctured with the biblical element":

> If that lexicon which is based on Holy Writ were any longer popular, one might with less difficulty define and denominate certain phenomenal men. As it is, one must turn to some authority not liable to the charge of being tinctured with the biblical element (p. 353).

Vere turns to the Bible to designate Claggart's "nature"; Melville turns to a Platonic tautology. But in both cases, the question arises, What does it mean to seal an explanation with a quotation? And what, in Vere's case, does it mean to refer a legal mystery to a religious text?

If Vere names the "absolute"—as opposed to the martial—by means of quotations and allusions, does this not suggest that the two alternative frames of reference within which judgment is possible are not nature and the king, but rather two types of textual authority: the Bible and the Mutiny Act? This is not to say that Vere is "innocently" choosing one text over another, but that the nature of "nature" in a legal context cannot be taken for granted. Even Thomas Paine, who is referred to by Melville in his function as proponent of "natural" human rights, cannot avoid grounding his concept on nature in biblical myth. In the very act of rejecting the authority of antiquity, he writes:

> The fact is, that portions of antiquity, by proving every thing, establish nothing. It is authority against authority all the way, till we come to the divine origin of the rights of man, at the Creation. Here our inquiries find a resting-place, and our reason finds a home.

The final frame of reference is neither the heart nor the gun, neither nature nor the king, but the authority of a sacred text. Authority seems to be nothing other than the vanishing-point of textuality. And nature is authority whose textual origins have been forgotten. Even behind the martial order of the world of the man-of-war, there lies a religious referent: the *Bellipotent*'s last battle is with a French ship called the *Athée*.

Judgment, then, would seem to ground itself in a suspension of the opposition between textuality and referentiality, just as politics can be seen as that which makes it impossible to draw the line between "language" and "life." Vere, indeed, is presented as a reader who does not recognize the "frontier" between "remote allusions" and current events:

> In illustrating of any point touching the stirring personages and events of the time he would be as apt to cite some historic character or incident of antiquity as he would be to cite from the moderns. He seemed unmindful of the circumstances that to his bluff company such remote allusions, however perti-nent they might really be, were altogether alien to men whose reading was mainly confined to the journals. But considerate-ness in such matters is not easy to natures constituted like Captain Vere's. Their honesty prescribes to them directness, sometimes far-reaching like that of a migratory fowl that in its flight never heeds when it crosses a frontier (p. 341).

Yet it is by inviting Billy Budd and John Claggart to "cross" the "frontier" between their proper territory and their superior's cabin, between the private and the political realms, that Vere unwittingly sets up the conditions for the narrative chiasmus he must judge.

As was noted earlier, Captain Vere's function, according to many critics, is to insert "ambiguity" into the story's "oversimplified" allegorical opposition. Yet, at the same time, it is Captain Vere who inspires the most vehement critical oppositions. In other words, he seems to mobilize simultaneously the seemingly contradictory forces of ambiguity and polarity.

In his median position between the Budd/Claggart opposition and the acceptance/irony opposition, Captain Vere functions as a focus for the conversion of polarity into ambiguity and back again. Interestingly, he plays exactly the same role in the progress of the plot. It is Vere who brings together the "innocent" Billy and the "guilty" Claggart in order to test the validity of Claggart's accusations, but he does so in such a way as to effect not a clarification but a reversal of places between guilt and innocence. Vere's fatherly words to Billy trigger the ambiguous deed upon which Vere must pronounce a verdict of "condemn *or* let go." Just as Melville's readers, faced with the ambiguity they themselves recognize as being provided by Vere, are quick to pronounce the captain vicious *or* virtuous, evil *or* just; so, too, Vere, who clearly perceives the "mystery" in the "moral dilemma" confronting him, must nevertheless reduce the situation to a binary opposition.

It would seem, then, that the function of judgment is to convert an ambiguous situation into a decidable one. But it does so by converting a difference *within* (Billy as divided between conscious submissiveness and unconscious hostility, Vere as divided between understanding father and military authority) into a difference *between* (between Claggart and Billy, between Nature and the King, between authority and criminality). A difference *between* opposing forces presupposes that the entities in conflict be knowable. A difference *within* one of the entities in question is precisely what problematizes the very *idea* of an entity in the first place, rendering the "legal point of view" inapplicable. In studying the plays of both ambiguity and binarity, Melville's story situates *its* critical difference neither within nor between, but in the *relation between the two* as the fundamental question of all human politics. The political context in *Billy Budd* is such that on all levels the differences *within* (mutiny on the warship, the French revolution as a threat to "lasting institutions," Billy's unconscious hostility) are subordinated to differences *between* (the *Bellipotent* vs. the *Athée*, England vs. France, murderer vs. victim). This is why Melville's choice of historical setting is so significant; the war between France and England at the time of the French Revolution is as striking an example of the simultaneous functioning of differences within and between as is the confrontation between Billy and Claggart in relation to their own internal divisions. War, indeed, is the absolute transformation of all differences into binary differences.

It would seem, then, that the maintenance of political authority requires that the law function as a set of rules for the regular, predictable misreading of the "difference within" as a "difference between." Yet if, as our epigraph from Plato suggests, law is thus defined in terms of its repression of ambiguity, then it is itself an overwhelming example of an entity based on a "difference within." Like Billy, the law, in attempting to eliminate its own "deadly space," can only inscribe itself in a space of deadliness.

In seeking to regulate the violent effects of difference, the political work of cognition is thus an attempt to situate that which must be eliminated. Yet in the absence of the possibility of knowing the locus and origin of violence, cognition itself becomes an act of violence. In terms of pure understanding, the drawing of a line between opposing entities does violence to the irreducible ambiguities that subvert the very possibility of determining the limits of what an "entity" is:

> Who in the rainbow can draw the line where the violet tint ends and the orange tint begins? Distinctly we see the difference of the colors, but where exactly does the first blendingly enter into the other? So with sanity and insanity. In pronounced cases there is no question about them. But in some supposed cases, in various degrees supposedly less pronounced, to draw the exact line of demarcation few will undertake, though for a fee becoming considerate some professional experts will. There is nothing nameable but that some men will, or undertake to, do it for pay (p. 379).

As an act, drawing a line is inexact and violent; and it also problematizes the very possibility of situating the "difference between" the judge and what is judged, between the interests of the "expert" and the truth of his expertise. What every act of judgment manifests is not the value of the object but the position of the judge within a structure of exchange. There is, in other words, no position from which to judge that would be outside the lines of force involved in the object judged.

But if judging is always a *partial* reading (in both senses of the word), is there a place for reading beyond politics? Are we, as Melville's readers, outside the arena in which power and fees are exchanged? If law is the forcible transformation of ambiguity into decidability, is it possible to read ambiguity *as such*, without that reading functioning as a political act?

Melville has something to say even about this. For there is a fourth reader in *Billy Budd*, one who "never interferes in aught and never gives advice" (p. 363): the old Dansker. A man of "few words, many wrinkles" and "the complexion of an antique parchment" (p. 347), the Dansker is the very picture of one who understands and emits ambiguous utterances. When asked by Billy for an explanation of his petty troubles, the Dansker says only, "Jemmy Legs [Claggart] is down on you" (p. 349). This interpretation, entirely accurate as a reading of Claggart's ambiguous behavior, is handed down to Billy without further explanation:

> Something less unpleasantly oracular he tried to extract; but
> the old sea Chiron, thinking perhaps that for the nonce he
> had sufficiently instructed his young Achilles, pursed his lips,
> gathered all his wrinkles together, and would commit himself
> to nothing further (p. 349).

As a reader who understands ambiguity yet refuses to "commit himself," the Dansker thus dramatizes a reading that attempts to be as cognitively accurate and performatively neutral as possible. Yet however neutral he tries to remain, the Dansker's reading does not take place outside the political realm; it is his very refusal to participate in it, whether by further instruction or by direct intervention, that leads to Billy's exclamation in the soup episode ("There now, who says Jemmy Legs is down on me?"). The transference of knowledge is no more innocent than the transference of power, for it is through the impossibility of finding a spot from which knowledge could be all-encompassing that the plays of political power proceed.

Just as the attempt to know without doing can itself function as a deed, the fact that judgment is always explicitly an act adds a further insoluble problem to its cognitive predicament. Since, as Vere points out, no judgment can take place in the "*Last* Assizes," no judge can ever pronounce a Last Judgment. In order to reach a verdict, Vere must determine the consequences not only of the fatal blow but also of his own verdict. Judgment is an act not only because it kills, but because it is in turn open to judgment:

"Can we not convict and yet mitigate the penalty?" asked the sailing master. . . .

"Gentlemen, were that clearly lawful for us under the circumstances, consider the consequences of such clemency. . . . To the people the foretopman's deed, however it be worded in the announcement, will be plain homicide committed in a flagrant act of mutiny. What penalty for that should follow, they know. But it does not follow. *Why*? They will ruminate. You know what sailors are. Will they not revert to the recent outbreak at the Nore?" (p. 389).

The danger is not only one of repeating the Nore mutiny, however. It is also one of forcing Billy, for all his innocence, to repeat his crime. Billy is a politically charged object from the moment he strikes his superior. He is no longer, and can never again be, plotless. If he were set free, he himself would be unable to explain why. As a focus for the questions and intrigues of the crew, he would be even less capable of defending himself than before, and would surely strike again. The political reading, as cognition, attempts to understand the past; as performance, it attempts to eliminate from the future any necessity for its own recurrence.

What this means is that every judge is in the impossible position of having to include the effects of his own act of judging within the cognitive context of his decision. The question of the nature of the type of historical causality that would govern such effects can neither be decided nor ignored. Because of his official position, Vere cannot choose to read in such a way that his reading would not be an act of political authority. But Melville shows in *Billy Budd* that authority consists precisely in the impossibility of containing the effects of its own application.

As a political allegory, Melville's *Billy Budd* is thus much more than a study of good and evil, justice and injustice. It is a dramatization of the twisted relations between knowing and doing, speaking and killing, reading and judging, which make political understanding and action so problematic. In the subtle creation of Claggart's "evil" out of a series of spaces in knowledge, Melville shoes that gaps in cognition, far from being mere absences, take on the performative power of true acts. The *force* of what is not known is all the more effective for not being perceived as such. The crew, which does not understand that it does not know, is no less performative a reader than the captain, who clearly perceives and represses the presence of "mystery." The legal order, which attempts to submit "brute force" to "forms, measured forms," can only eliminate violence by transforming violence into the final authority. And cognition, which perhaps begins as a power play against the play of power, can only increase, through its own elaboration, the range of what it tries to dominate. The "deadly space" or "difference" that runs through *Billy Budd* is not located between knowledge and action, performance and cognition. It is that which, within cognition, functions as an act; it is that which, within action, prevents us from ever knowing whether what we hit coincides with what we understand. And this is what makes the meaning of Melville's last work so *striking*.

Suspense and Tautology
in "Benito Cereno"

Eric J. Sundquist

> *When I take a retrospective view of my life, I cannot find in my soul, that I have ever done anything to deserve such misery and ingratitude as I have suffered at different periods, and in general, from the very persons to whom I have rendered the greatest services.*
>
> AMASA DELANO, *Narrative of Voyages and Travels in the Northern and Southern Hemispheres* (1817)

At the end of "Benito Cereno" in a scene presented "retrospectively, and irregularly" [*Great Short Works of Herman Melville*, ed. Warner Berthoff (New York: Harper & Row, 1969), p. 313; all further references to "Benito Cereno" are to this edition], the American Captain Delano once more confronts the spiritually wasted Benito Cereno, but he finds in the melancholy gloom that continues to descend upon the Spaniard a mystery just as baffling as his strange conduct aboard the *San Dominick*:

> "But the past is passed; why moralize upon it? Forget it. See, yon bright sun has forgotten it all, and the blue sea, and the blue sky; these have turned over new leaves."
>
> "Because they have no memory," [Cereno] dejectedly replied; "because they are not human."
>
> "But these mild trades that now fan your check, do they not come with a human-like healing to you? Warm friends, steadfast friends are the trades."

From *Glyph: Johns Hopkins Textual Studies*, no. 8 (1981). © 1981 by The Johns Hopkins University Press.

"With their steadfastness they but waft me to my tomb, Señor," was the foreboding response.

"You are saved," cried Captain Delano, more and more astonished and pained; "you are saved: what has cast such a shadow upon you?"

"The negro" (p. 314).

The silence that follows this conversation, echoing the moments of suspended or suppressed power that animate Melville's whole tale, leaves the American and the Spaniard poised once again in the posture of flawed communication and failed communion that defines their relationship throughout the story of the slave revolt aboard the *San Dominick*. And it leaves the reader suspended more emphatically than ever between the apparent insensitivity of Delano and the shadow of moral complicity that has enveloped Don Benito — suspended, that is, between possible responses to the revolt that seem in utter opposition but which may nonetheless be dangerously, antagonistically equal. The last conversation takes place chronologically between the slave rebellion and the court proceedings; but by delaying it until the end of the tale and forcing us to consider now and in retrospect the mystery (of guilt) that remains unsolved within the mystery (of the revolt) that has been solved, Melville's narrative form continues to hold in precarious suspense the balked implementations of commanding authority and suppressed powers of correct interpretation that control both our response and that of the characters to the actions that create and contain the rebellion of slave against master.

The shadow of the confrontation between Delano and Cereno, like the shadow of "the negro" that both joins and separates them, falls in retrospect between the mystery story and the legal depositions in a way that also brings fiction and history, tale and documents, into poised confrontation, merged but separated in an act of suspension. Such a characterization of Melville's narrative form is appropriate since the mystery story itself and to a less immediately evident extent the complete rendering of the tale are infused with dramatic suspense — so much so that it has led Richard Chase, for example, to speak quite rightly of the "universe" depicted as one "poised upon a present that continually merges with the opulent debris of a dying past and reaches into a vacant and terrifying future," a universe suspended in the rituals of meaning between "necessity and chance," "reason and madness," "speech and silence," or "communication and isolation" in which men "must try to communicate with each other with half-formed, half-intended gestures — a universe in which consciousness is completely involved and yet completely alienated." Chase's nearly frenzied proliferation of terms irreconcilable yet almost equivalent — to which he might well have added the pairings "black and white" or "slave and master" — is an index of the haunting power of "Benito Cereno." This power encompasses the suppressed actions of revolt and recognition among the characters, the cagey manipulation of Melville's narrative voice, and the fusion in narrative form between historical documents and invented fictions; and it is one which in its generation of ironic effects, I want to argue, can best be described as tautological, creating as it does a moral riddle whose possible interpretations, like the narrator and characters themselves, merge and react, or verge unwittingly on stances of identity and communion that can never be fulfilled, remaining in the end separate but equal.

I. The Shadowy Tableau

By reading the last perilous dialogue between Captain Delano and Benito Cereno at the outset, we risk violating the act of delayed or suspended remembrance that Melville's deliberate unfolding of this critical scene "retrospectively, and irregularly" in the course of his narrative places so crucially before us. But "Benito Cereno" is a mystery story that must be read more than once, and the act of retrospection, with its attendant complications of human memory that Delano seems easily to put aside, serves to define the "shadow" of guilt created in a story whose actions take place in 1799 but still suspended in the process of its descent over the American conscience of 1855. The invitation to rest comfortably in the blue sky and sunshine of the legal resolutions set forth in the deposition, as the captain of the *Bachelor's Delight* does, is one to which the American reader of Melville's day might have been particularly susceptible, and one which more recent criticism of "Benito Cereno," in its confessed need for the "symmetry of form" that Melville himself felt was unattainable in fiction, has in its own way accepted. While some readers early and late dismiss the legal documents as simply irrelevant, or as an unnecessary flaw resulting from Melville's hasty composition or his attempt to stretch his commercial reward from *Putnam's Magazine*, a majority have seen in those documents an approximation of the full moral burden of his tale, a burden which Delano escapes and to which Benito Cereno succumbs in the muted finale. Returning the tale to the actual history from which it emerged, and at the same time reconstituting the social and political conventions threatened by the revolt aboard the *San Dominick* and held in absolute suspension by the mystery play engendered in Delano's consciousness, the deposition acts retrospectively to explain and endorse, in stately legal phrases, the urgent suppression of the slaves' revolt.

But the explanation, as Warner Berthoff notes, becomes itself a part of Melville's "extended narrative riddle," a "highly stylized" version of the preceding events that by "delayed double-exposure" allows us to "circle back through the cruxes and important details" of a mystery tale whose retellings we relish. And yet far from allowing "the mechanism of our encounter" with the mystery "to run down, to trail off into 'anticlimax' . . . [and thus] act to contain its disturbing force," as Berthoff argues it does, the deposition gathers those disturbing forces into a ritual of suppression that climaxes in the execution of Babo, the wasting death of Benito Cereno, and the frightening insensitivity of Captain Delano. It is in the "retrospective" tag ending that the tale and court documents, like Cereno and Delano, are brought into poised confrontation once again; and as I will want to suggest, Melville's narrative form alerts us to what may be a dangerous equality in that confrontation, one that recapitulates and enlarges the threat of tautology that envelops the entire tale. If the deposition limits and contains the violence, and ultimately the moral significance, of the events barely held in check in the first part of Melville's story, it does so incompletely; for the final scenes of the executed Babo and the ruined Benito Cereno emerge as a "shadow" which the language of the court and the coldblooded documents of history cannot fully *contain*. The rituals of the court do not rescue Benito Cereno from the shadow of "the negro," and neither do they recall the reader to a position from which he, like Delano in the climactic moment when a "flash of revelation" illuminates "in unanticipated clearness" the riddle of the *San Dominick* (p. 295), can comfortably reflect on Melville's irony. Rather, in the sudden illumination of Captain Delano that occurs "with such involutions of rapidity, that past, present, and future seemed one" (p. 294)—in a vision both clarified and nonetheless seriously flawed—there rests the wrenching dilemma that the reader participates in presently and retrospectively each time he reads and reflects upon Melville's tale.

It is important to emphasize the element of retrospection not simply because the style of the mystery story depends on it in obvious ways, and not only because the court documents strive to pacify or repress the memories that the form of the narrative asks us to look back on—imaging *now*, as we do, the murderous revolt and the tortured anguish of Benito Cereno during Delano's presence—but also because the crucial scene between the two captains that Melville chooses to present retrospectively defines the moral imperative that brings the shadow of the past insistently before us today, even as in 1855 it brought the completely relevant events of 1799 and the shadow of "the negro" before an audience presumably filled with Americans like Captain Delano, suspending those events in a gesture of irreducible tension. We need presently to consider the way in which retrospection is intimately tied to the problem of fiction's relationship with history, and consequently to the tension between the metaphoric and the literal, or the ritual and the actual, that "Benito Cereno" continually engages, but should first take note of what may be an obvious quality: that Melville's tales, more so than his novels, seem virtually to live in our memories with a haunting force that somehow exceeds the small compass of the dramas they describe. This force derives in part from Melville's disciplined exploitation of the potentials for sudden irony and expressive silence afforded by the short tale, as well as from his further exploitation of the links between fiction and memory so important in American fiction, whose writers have often found their best powers in troubled or revolutionary confrontations with a past that remains vexingly present even as it passes into history. The power of the past to impinge almost uncontrollably upon the present, or upon a future holding forth its implied freedoms and creative potentials, has been a consistent concern of American authors and moreover of their audiences, which of necessity live in that future and direct and qualify those potentials, making of them their own memorable past. If "Benito Cereno," like other notable American texts of the nineteenth century—Emerson's essays, Hawthorne's *The House of the Seven Gables*, and Twain's *Huckleberry Finn*, for example—tends to live as vividly in our memories as in actual encounter and seems to haunt us so in retrospect, it is in part because it fully exploits, by reflected narrative action and by the formal suspension of moments of crisis, impending problems at once relegated to the historical past but nonetheless alive in the fictional present.

In order to judge more carefully these formal strategies and to show more evidently their operation in "Benito Cereno," it may be best to consider a passage that comes early on but which, like so many of Melville's eventfully controlled passages of descriptive commentary, opens up in retrospect into a more forceful commentary on the full structure of the tale. "Always upon first boarding a large and populous ship at sea," the narrative voice declares, attempting to record "some such influence" as must have affected Captain Delano on first boarding the *San Dominick*,

> the impression varies in a peculiar way from that produced by first entering a strange house with strange inmates in a strange land. Both house and ship . . . hoard from view their interiors till the last moment; but in the case of the ship there is this addition: that the living spectacle it contains, upon its sudden and complete disclosure, has, in contrast with the blank ocean which zones it, something of the effect of enchantment. The ship seems unreal; these strange costumes, gestures, and faces, but a shadowy tableau just emerged from the deep, which must directly receive back what it gave (p. 242).

The passage is instructive not only because it offers an instance of the perplexing distance between the narrator and Delano, a distance that continually collapses and expands in the various metaphors offered and retracted from Delano's "point of view," but also because the "shadowy tableau" emerging from and returning to the deep contains in miniature the "shadow" of moral complicity first cast off in the deposition but suddenly reconstituted in the retrospective ending of the tale. In addition, and perhaps more importantly, the emergence and retraction of the shadowy tableau at the same time defines the dramatic structure of Melville's invented tale itself, which emerges in fictional form from chapter 18 of Amasa Delano's *Narrative of Voyages and Travels in the Northern and Southern Hemispheres* (1817) but which suddenly returns, in the plagiarized language of the legal deposition, to the buried and, for Melville, publicly unacknowledged depths of history. The relationship between fiction and history is more complex for Melville than my analogy immediately suggests; and in fact the last conversation between the two captains, looking back to a time after the revolt but prior to the deposition, serves to show how incompletely the story does return to the rhetorical resources of its historical account, generating instead, with a further and more complex "effect of enchantment," a shadow of guilt insufficiently suppressed. But the passage also defines a kind of movement that occurs locally and repeatedly in scenes as they are perceived by Delano aboard the *San Dominick*, and in a way that makes the effective relationship between suspense and retrospection, and consequently between experience and judgment, more urgent.

Clearly, appearances aboard the *San Dominick* are deceptive: slave is master, and master is slave; black is white, and white is black, as it were, and Captain Delano's every interpretation of the events before him is ironically incorrect — or so it seems. Continually he tries "to break one charm" only to be "becharmed anew" (p. 269), as he gets progressively enveloped in a vapor of "currents [that] spin one's head around almost as much as they do the ship" (p. 267). The effect of enchantment these passages suggest is progressive, however, and that sense of progress into a deepening and nearly suffocating mystery is important as it compels the reader's attention ever more forcefully and as it brings Delano closer and closer to the melancholy depression of Benito Cereno, utterly immobilized in what is but the theatrical posture of his former authority. The incipient merger of the two characters, progressively suggested but never allowed to take place — and in the end radically denied by their completely divergent views of the significance of the slave revolt — is a measure of the operative irony in the tale, an irony that finally goes beyond the revelation of apparent deception to verge more closely upon outright tautology, suspending meaning between possibilities that are not simply exclusive and opposite but rather dangerously equal. The atmosphere of suspense impels the mystery story at a fundamental level; it pervades the ghostly and dreamlike setting of the slave ship stranded in symbolic significance between Europe and America and enveloped in a mysterious "gray" calm that seems almost a conspiracy of nature; and it defines the stymied crisis aboard the ship in which the authority of each of three possible "captains" in asserted and restrained in frozen confrontation — Delano's because he is a guest aboard the *San Dominick* and must defer to Benito Cereno's ostensible command, Cereno's because his authority has been usurped by Babo, and Babo's because he must continue to play the part of the slave while maturing his plot against Delano's ship. Acting in a form of circular displacement, the three possible sources of authority are equal to the extent that they each require abdication, reserve, or suppression in order to maintain the semblance of control. Authority — like the drifting ship, the simmering revolt, the guarded speech of the possible commanders, and the language of the narrative that simultaneously unfolds and withholds the drama before us — is caught in a point of crisis and held in precarious suspension.

In this respect the suspense inherent in Melville's mystery story goes beyond attachment to the kind of suspended judgment we might be inclined to attribute to Delano's innocent or blinded point of view, for it is clear early on that we are not exactly in Delano's shoes, but rather are suspended between "the sardonic, third-person intelligence" (as John Seelye describes the narrator) that offers an extravagant and increasingly potent array of figurative clues and the American captain, to whom the very creation of those clues is often ascribed but who nonetheless fails, with mounting frustration, to interpret them correctly. Stranded as we are between a character who is, after all, Melville's mock creation and a nearly parodic generation of portentous symbols, similes, and metaphors also of Melville's creation, we are prevented from residing comfortably in either one or the other intelligence and from granting one or the other a full measure of authority. Or one might simply say that Melville the "author" fully participates in the suspension of authority: like Benito Cereno, "eating of his own words, even as he ever seemed eating of his own heart" (p. 276), he checks his powers while displaying them and renders his judgment in the very act of withholding it. We need to stress Melville's involvement with the suspension of authority because it is crucial to the function of metaphor — and ultimately of "fiction" — in the tale and to the effective implication of the reader in the moral complexities that acceptance or rejection of those metaphors entails as they continually explode and decline, page after page, precipitously closing in on the true state of affairs but never quite containing it.

The difficulty with judging Delano's perceptions lies in the complex relationship between him and the narrative voice, which moves silently in and out of the captain's point of view, engaging and promoting his suspicions, then retracting them in sudden dismissals. Since Melville seems to have taken his central metaphor for the relationship between Benito Cereno and Babo from a passage in Delano's *Narrative* in which he describes the original Cereno as a man "frightened at his own shadow," it would be appropriate to speak of the narrative voice, which dictates to Delano as surely as Babo does to Benito Cereno, as itself a kind of "shadow," at once merged with but partially suspended above or outside his conscious point of view. The merger between the two figures is constantly suggested but never completely realized, and perhaps the most accurate way of characterizing the narrative voice would be to call it a voice of the "unconscious," an embodied reservoir of those impressions that seem to take their cue from the few symbolic constructs that mark in ironic projection the true character of the ship — the masked satyr of the sternpiece, the concealed figurehead of Aranda's skeleton and its chalked admonition, "follow your leader" (p. 241) — and spring momentarily to Delano's mind before lapsing back into the shadowy region from which they have emerged. The passages that might lead us to characterize the narrative voice in this way are numerous and include, for example, nearly all the instances of narration that set the scene and define the ship as a "whitewashed monastery" with a load of monks, a "superannuated" palace under a "decline of masters," and a virtual skeleton, hearse, or drifting sarcophagus (pp. 240-42, 268).

There are instances that will require closer attention, but it is worth considering at this point one scene in which Delano seems most clearly to articulate to himself the possible interpretations that might account for Don Benito's odd behavior. While Benito Cereno and Babo are engaged in one of their private "whisperings," Delano thinks he perceives a sign from the young Spanish sailor, whose eye passes suggestively from Delano to the "two whisperers," and he immediately suspects that he is the subject of the conversation, a suspicion that is "unaccountable, except on one of two suppositions" about Benito Cereno — "innocent lunacy, or wicked imposture" (pp. 257-58). The truth in fact falls between the two possibilities; but Delano, dismissing the possibility of lunacy, inclines at this point to suspect treachery, imagining that "under the aspect of infantile weakness, the most savage energies might be couched — those velvets of the Spaniard but the silky paw to his fangs." His surmise in retrospect applies perfectly to Babo of course, but the narrative immediately continues in a telling and representative fashion: "From no train of thought did these fancies come; not from within, but from without; suddenly, too, and in one throng, like hoar frost; yet as soon to vanish as the mild sun of Captain Delano's good-nature regained its meridian" (p. 258). The train of thought, coming from without as though from a dictating voice, exists for us clearly on the page — more clearly, it appears, than it does even in Delano's mind, where it has seemed to unfold. Even more characteristic is the scene in which Delano observes a sailor whose haggard face seems to suggest a kind of "criminality" that cannot quite be determined, "since, as intense heat and cold, though unlike, produce like sensations, so innocence and guilt, when, through casual association with mental pain, stamping any visible impress, use one seal — a hacked one." Once more the passage looks ahead in commentary upon later events, but the narrator immediately retracts this train of thought from Delano — "Not again that this reflection occurred to Captain Delano at the time, charitable man as he was" — and notes that he rather was only "insensible . . . operated upon by certain general notions which, while disconnecting pain and abashment from virtue, invariably link them with vice" (p. 266). Again the narrative voice projects a metaphor that appears to belong consciously to Delano, existing on the page as in the window of his imagination, but then partially withdraws it, leaving the shadow of suggested meaning suspended between the mind that embodies and the voice that creates. The narrator's voice continually forms connections, sympathies, and judgments that either do not occur at all to Delano, though they at first appear to, or which at best get articulated insensibly, unconsciously, or retrospectively. Delano's consciousness is thus a trap for the reader not simply because his insensitivity and naiveté are presented as a moral challenge, but moreover because the cunning narrative voice lures the reader in only to discount suddenly the perceptions it has projected, insidiously displacing the possibility of a rebellion by the slaves onto Delano's suspicions of a malicious plot engineered by Benito Cereno. Again and again the "shadowy tableaux" erupting in Delano's consciousness are swallowed up by the depths from which they have emerged, as the narrative voice, in near mimicry of the haunted Spaniard, "eats its own words."

The implementing structure of such dismissals is absolutely central to the maintenance of suspense, however, in the immediately obvious way of presenting then repressing a series of clues that counter the crude racial metaphors of pastoral and domestic tranquillity that occur to Delano as he observes the slaves (e.g., pp. 267–68, 278–79); and in the perhaps less obvious but more telling way in which we are forced to recognize that structuring as a retrospective device by which the narrative asserts then denies its observations, expressing in abdication the authority it has just assumed. And yet, of course, the "shadows" of suggestion presented by the narrative voice are no more completely resubmerged than the shadow of terror — the shadow of "the negro" — that hangs over Don Benito at the tale's end. Rather, they are suspended, frozen in the act of retrospection taking place on the page of the text and in the psychological space that is neither Delano's nor the narrator's but more properly *ours*, who inhabit the strange distance between the two and engage, by reading, in the acts of projection and dismissal dictated by the narrative voice. The story we read is as completely "dictated" to us as the "fictitious story" of fevers and calms is "dictated" by Babo to Benito Cereno for presentation to Delano, and as completely as Cereno's account of the revolt aboard the *San Dominick* is dictated to the court for presentation, in ceremonious indirect speech, to the public. It is important to raise the implicit connection between the narrator and Babo as partially concealed and at times virtually silent dictators, a connection that will require more detailed examination with regard to Melville's depiction of Babo as an "artist," because we are as cunningly manipulated by the narrator as Benito Cereno is by Babo, to such an extent in fact that the last tormented image we are presented as Delano leaves the *San Dominick*, joined hand in hand with Cereno across the supporting and mediating figure of "the black's body" (p. 293), is one wholly appropriate to the tenuous relationship between the reader and Delano, joined but separated by the conspiring voice of the narrator exercising his authority in the very act of holding it in suspension. The importance of these parallel configurations will perhaps be clarified if we think of the image of the two captains linked to the last by their ever-present slave and master as a metaphor—a metaphor for the suspense that governs the book and a figure for metaphor itself, which suspends two significations, two potentially equal authorities, separating and joining them by the "shadow" of meaning that falls between.

II. The Play of the Barber

The illusion of equality, in the rituals of life and in the materials of art, is one that may be central to Melville's imaginative vision in "Benito Cereno"; but if it is so, it may also offer a consequent challenge to the simple—or one might say, "innocent"—irony usually attributed to Melville's tale. The "dread of tautology," Melville remarks at one point in *Pierre*, is "the continual torment of some earnest minds," and though tautology nowhere in "Benito Cereno" reaches the ennervating pitch it does in Melville's incest-romance, it is nonetheless important to the narrative unfolding of evidence about the mystery with which Delano is confronted. Unlike irony, which by deception, insinuation, or bald presumption revolts against the authority of one meaning to proclaim the authority of another, tautology asserts the virtual equivalence of potentially different authorities or meanings. It does so by rhetorical mimicry—by an actual or fully implied reproduction of phrases or gestures—or by bringing two meanings into such approximation as to collapse the distinction between them without literally doing so. Tautology, since it suggests but prohibits identity, offers an absurd paradox that necessarily "contains" irony; and one might say that it does so by subverting the revolutionary intent of irony, stiffling its import and suspending its achieved effect in forms separate but equal.

To speak of irony and tautology in terms of revolt and suspension is wholly appropriate in the case of "Benito Cereno" since those figures, whether as act or as rhetorical gesture, are so much at the heart of Melville's tale and text. By failing to understand the ironic import of his own remarks to Benito Cereno, and moreover by articulating (through a narrative voice that seems the tormenting mirror of his mind) suspicions that move closer and closer to the literal truth of events aboard the *San Dominick*, Delano unwittingly participates in a continued act of suppressed revolt against belief in the appearances presented to him, and by doing so reflects in interpretive action the reader's equally frustrated position. The recognitions by Delano that occur almost but not quite, because they are either unintentional or barely conscious, work to prevent the completion of irony and to delay the proper response of the reader, who if not on a first reading, certainly in retrospect and on subsequent readings fully apprehends the tautological character of the American Captain's carefully manipulated point of view. As though he were Benito Cereno, "painfully turning in the half embrace of his servant" and master Babo (p. 250), the reader turns in the half embrace of Melville's painfully revealed figures, explicitly offered then retracted through the mediating innocence of Captain Delano, which constantly disarms the revolts in rhetoric that adhere to the revolt that has virtually taken place aboard the ship.

The function of tautology in *Benito Cereno* can perhaps better be described with reference to a scene whose full implications we need to consider in a moment — the shaving scene in which Delano watches the barbering Babo flourish his razor at the neck of the cringing Don Benito with the gentle but excruciating admonition, "now, master . . . now, master," and cannot "resist the vagary, that in the black he saw a headsman, and in the white a man at the block. But this," the narrator adds, "was one of those antic conceits, appearing and vanishing in a breath, from which, perhaps, the best regulated mind is not always free" (p. 280). The scene of imminent decapitation that occurs to Delano as an "antic conceit" is hardly the first instance in the tale in which a metaphor, springing to mind almost inexplicably, contains a relevant significance immediately dismissed not so much by Delano himself as by the peculiar narrative voice that speaks through him. In this case, however, the implied decapitation is in fact more true, more real, as it were, than the actual shaving that takes place; that is, the suggested metaphor falls into such close equivalence with the actual event as to be nearly synonymous with it. The scene is not simply ironic, but rather verges on tautology in such a way that the act of shaving — replete with ceremonial trappings that include the flag of Spain as a barber's apron and a barber's chair that seems "some grotesque engine of torment" (p. 278)—is not just a symbol of Babo's usurped authority but its virtual embodiment, one that releases and contains its significance in the act of holding it poised, like Babo's blade "suspended for an instant" near "the Spaniard's lank neck" (p. 280), at razor's edge. Both the physical scene and the suggested metaphors of threat here conspire to form a concentrated ritual that recapitulates the torturous drama aboard the *San Dominick* and defines a scene of judgment at once exterior and interior. It is in Melville's withdrawal of that suggested significance, however, that its simultaneously enacted and withheld power is most clearly felt. The "antic conceit," issuing suddenly from an apparent relaxation of control in Delano's "best regulated mind," is a form of revolt against perceptive and rhetorical constraint: as a revolutionary gesture—and moreover one that is nearly involuntary—the conceit, the suggested metaphor, parallels the actual revolt that has occurred but which is held temporarily in abeyance. The suspension or deferral of completion in the revolt that Delano's presence aboard the ship provokes is echoed in his own deferred acceptance of the conceit presented so boldly to him.

That suspension depends, as we have noticed, on the precarious posture of innocence or naiveté of a man who with absolutely no irony can ask himself, "who would murder Amasa Delano? His conscience is clean" (p. 272); and before more fully accounting for the relationship between Delano and the narrative voice—a relationship that is charged with suspense and which virtually takes on the function of metaphor in the tale—we need to consider the comic powers of suppressed revelation, and thus the potential for tautological conceit, which that naiveté makes possible. The grotesque exhilaration that the shaving scene provides, recapitulating and redirecting with ritual precision the scenes of near-recognition and stymied observation built up throughout the tale, depends on Delano's being confronted with a representation of the true character of events, a representation that he at once articulates and misconceives, rendering in language painfully accurate a meaning opposite or irrelevant to his intention. Various scenes in which his supposed train of thought is asserted then retracted, or in which the narrator merges with then withdraws from Delano's point of view, inform the tension that the shaving scene maintains at the very edge of humorous terror. But the effect of the shaving scene is more pointedly prepared for by several specific instances of conversation between Delano and Cereno where the question of the narrator's control is less evident. Not the most powerful, but perhaps rhetorically the most revealing, is the first scene in which the chained Atufal appears before Benito Cereno in the mock ritual of asking pardon. His attention directed by Babo to the key suspended around Cereno's neck, Delano smiles and remarks, "'So, Don Benito—padlock and key—significant symbols, truly.'" The symbols are significant as they define the tale's pervasive irony and moreover—as I will want to argue with respect to the deposition, which is presented as a "key" to the preceding events—as they define the function of metaphor as a device that both fuses and segregates potentially equivalent meanings; but at this point it is important to note that the comic power of the exchanged remarks depends on the Spaniard's lapsing into yet another fit of despondency, one apparently produced by his taking Delano's statement as a "malicious reflection" on his fragile authority, but one delivered by a man both he and we know to be, in the narrator's words, "incapable of satire or irony" (pp. 256–57).

Here, as elsewhere, the irony is the narrator's, and its comic exploitation issues from a flawed communication for whose irony neither of the two captains is explicitly responsible, Cereno feeling the keen thrust of an irony that goes far beyond malicious intent, and Delano having intended no irony or satire at all. As a form of irony whose achieved completion can only be retrospective, the significance of Delano's remarks depends upon his being innocent in intention and thus unwittingly participating in that powerful species of the comic that Freud finds to stand nearest to the joke in its structure—the naive. "The naive occurs," Freud notes, "if someone completely disregards an inhibition because it is not present in him," or in other words, if his statement is not *intended* as a joke. In the case of a naive remark, "an inhibitory expenditure which we usually make suddenly becomes unintelligible . . . [and] is discharged by laughter." Since "none of the characteristics of the naive exist except in the apprehension of the person who hears it," not in the person who thinks "he has used his means of expression and trains of thought normally and simply," the listener alone obtains the pleasure brought about by "the lifting of inhibitions." The implementing structure of the naive is thus a simple one, and yet it raises a number of interesting questions for our understanding of "Benito Cereno," not least because the lifting of inhibitory or repressive forces is what the tale is thoroughly about, and no less because it alerts us to a way in which the element of suspense continues to operate even more impressively on subsequent readings of the story, when our identification with Delano is a more troubled one, owing to our knowledge of the mystery's outcome.

Since our apprehension of the naive depends upon entering into the psychical processes of the person making the remark and feeling the thrust of a joke or irony he is unaware of—a process displayed in the narrative voice that often functions as though it were Delano's unconscious—we may be able to bring the naive even closer to the joke proper, which often seems to form itself "involuntarily," as Freud finds, when one "drops a train of thought for a moment," which "then suddenly emerges from the unconscious as a joke." The comic function of the naive in "Benito Cereno" would appear to fuse itself quite comfortably with the unconscious process of joking, for though Delano's intention may be said to be empty, the narrator's clearly is not, but rather presents itself virtually *as* the train of thought ascribed to Delano but which only we fully apprehend.

Don Benito is no more able to respond to Delano's unintended irony—that is, to acknowledge the lifting of inhibitions by laughter—than he is able to signal to Delano the true character of events aboard the ship: instead, he lapses into one or another fit of depression, tortured as much by Delano's incomprehension as he is by Babo's devious control. The comedy that we apprehend is thus a function of both Delano's empty intent and Cereno's failed response, and the precarious standoff or suspension of commanding authorities generated by the events of the story is supported and rendered all the more excruciating by the standoff that takes place in the interrupted function of the comic: the lifting of inhibitions occurs only in the reader, again and again, and yet its very repetition augments the urgency of its constant reformation and dispersal, to the point that one might well speak of the reader's own position as a kind of enslavement or tormented constraint. The relevance of these considerations will be more apparent if we take note of a late interview between Delano and Cereno, after the shaving scene and the luncheon, when Delano once again remarks on the ritual appearance of Atufal:

> "Don Benito," said he, "I give you joy; the breeze will hold, and will increase. By the way, your tall man and time-piece, Atufal, stands without. By your order, of course?"
>
> Don Benito recoiled, as if at some bland satirical touch, delivered with such adroit garnishy of good breeding as to present no handle for retort.
>
> He is like one flayed alive, thought Captain Delano; where may one touch him without causing a shrink? (p. 289).

For the obvious reasons we have just noted, Benito Cereno can find "no handle for retort" to any of Delano's remarks, in this case once again because the irony is neither intended nor does it permit an acknowledgement of reception. Cereno's response in such scenes consists either of fainting and silence or, at most, a shocked repetition of Delano's words, as in the early scene in which Delano unwittingly speaks of Alexandro Aranda's remains:

> "Were your friend's remains now on board this ship, Don Benito, not thus strangely would the mention of his name affect you."
> "On board this ship?" echoed the Spaniard. Then, with horrified gestures, as directed against some spectre, he unconsciously fell into the ready arms of his attendant (p. 254).

Benito Cereno's "echoing" of Delano's words, his repetition of them, is the only possible retort, and as such it offers a further clue to the way in which the comedy of the naive works in "Benito Cereno" and to the way in which Melville's irony verges continually upon a form of tautology. Both Delano and Cereno are presented with remarks or signals of one kind or another to which they are unable, for different reasons, to respond. We need eventually to consider the fact that these flawed or stiffled responses contribute to the merging of their characters that takes place over the course of the story but should note first that such standoffs, painfully comic in their involvement with the suspended rebellion that the story at once unfolds and holds in abeyance, are reflexive in action, enigmatic mirrorings that block the interpretation of, or response to, *evident* meaning by, as it were, handing it back to the one who speaks or acts it out. By virtual repetition, by fainting or silence, or by the troubled assent of "'doubtless, doubtless'" (pp. 253, 284), Benito Cereno "hands back" Delano's remarks to him as surely as Delano, in the famous scene in which he is presented a complicated knot by the aged sailor with the sudden and perplexing challenge, "'Undo it, cut it, quick,'" stands momentarily transfixed, "knot in hand, and knot in head," and then "unconsciously" hands it back to one of the elderly slaves (p. 271). The knot is so obviously a symbolic clue to the complexities aboard the ship that no critic can bypass it, and yet none has seemed to untangle its full implications. The nearly absurd exchange of remarks that precedes the challenge —

> "What are you knotting there, my man?"
> "The knot," was the brief reply, without looking up.

"So it seems; but what is it for?"

"For some one else to undo," muttered back the old man (p. 270).

— makes the knot's function so evident as to be ridiculous. Like the shaving scene, the conversation about the knot is a tableau whose figurative message so closely approaches the literal that its unfolding takes the form of tautology. And like the naively unintentional satiric thrusts of Delano himself, the knot in this case offers *him* no handle for retort. We are prompted to speak of the handling of the knot as a scene of tautology because it indicates the way in which tautology defines a situation in which presented meanings or signals are both the "same" and yet separated or suspended so as to act in a fashion one might call "tense" or "taut," and more peripherally because it calls out attention to the interest inherent in the archaic noun *taut*, which means "mat" or "tangle." The tangle in hand and the tangle in head are virtually the same to Delano — they are tangles, knots, or enigmas that offer and swallow up their meaning at the same time. Like the events aboard the ship and like the story itself, they offer something, one might say, that both *is* and *is not*, an irony that has no handle for retort and is thus transfigured into tautology.

The relationship between *knot* and *not* is perhaps evident to the point of humorous absurdity, but in the context of Melville's tale it gains its fullest power from the extraordinary proliferation of double negatives in the narrative description of Cereno's apparent actions and Delano's various trains of thought concerning them, suspending that thought between the rational and the unconscious, the deliberate and the unintentional. The instances of the double negative are numerous, but in almost all cases they are rhetorical embodiments of information or assessments that are at once asserted and denied — or to put it another way, of a rebellion in consciousness or language that takes place almost but not quite and thus remains in suspension. As in one of the "not unlikely" possibilities of Cereno's evil designs that occurs to Delano, for example, or immediately after this suspicion in the "not uncongenial" passing of his mind "from its own entaglements to those of the hemp" (p. 270), Delano's naiveté both promotes and checks his approach to the truth, making the *not* a virtual *knot* not fully untangled. The double negative is a localized version of the effect generated throughout by the precarious relationship between the narrative voice and the consciousness of Delano, a small retrospective action that asserts the formation of a suspicion or interpretation then partially withdraws it, creating in short compass an irony that is suggested but allowed neither completion nor proper handle for retort. "Not unlikely," "not unbewildered," "not unpleased," "not unaffected," "not without," for example, and the equally proliferate allied expression "could not but," all support and extend the pervasive "seems," "likes," and "as ifs" in the story that question nearly every act of Delano's consciousness just as he questions the reality of the events before him. The subtle distance between *is* and *is not* as between master and slave or between white and black, defines the shadowed gray area falling between, and yoking together, two poles in metaphor or two halves of irony, and forms the ground the reader treads in "Benito Cereno," a ground "every inch" of which (to borrow one of Cereno's final remarks to Delano) has been "mined into honey-combs" (p. 313) as perilously brittle as the decaying ship's balustrade, which at one point gives in to Delano's weight "like charcoal" (p. 269).

Scenes, roles, events, and suspicions that are and are not, or in which there are produced exclusive but nonetheless "like sensations," as of innocence and guilt, keep "Benito Cereno" poised in a barely suppressed revolutionary gesture, one that expresses the virtual equivalence of possibilities in a cunning narrative form that seems to duplicate the prior navigation of the doomed *San Dominick*, which "like a man lost in the woods, more than once . . . had doubled upon her own track" (p. 250). The narrative voice expresses, by both suggesting and containing, the rebellion that cannot be completed; and its own containment of Delano's consciousness at the point of explosive possibility brings the narrative by analogous form into closer and closer coincidence with the revolt on board the ship, creating in the reader, as in Delano, "a fatality not to be withstood," in which "all his former distrusts [sweep] through him" in "images far swifter than these sentences" (p. 292). And like the dramatic presentations of the chained Atufal, the striking at intervals of the ship's flawed bell, and the seemingly "coincidental" activities of the oakum-pickers, the singing negresses, and the threatening hatchet-polishers, whose work at one point seems to "strike up . . . as in ominous comment on the white stranger's thoughts" (p. 261), the narrative voice performs an act of ritual control, regulating and containing actions of imminent revolt in which the ceremonial may at any moment give way to the actual, in which roles threaten to be reversed and the figurative threatens to become recognized as the literal. The most elaborate ritual of all, of course, is the court deposition, which reasserts the control of white masters that has been overturned and suspended throughout the tale and which, I will want to suggest, also functions as a pole of metaphor or a half of irony with respect to the mystery story that precedes it. But the fullest and most haunting ritual in the story itself is the shaving scene, which we have touched on but whose function is perhaps now more apparent.

The "antic conceit" of imperial decapitation that occurs to Delano as a "vagary" he cannot "resist," springing from that "best regulated mind" constantly regulated and penetrated by the narrative voice, so closely approximates truth as to bring the metaphoric and the literal into a tautological relationship. And in fact, the drawing of "Babo's first blood," rather than dissipating the suspense only increases it, as Benito Cereno's nervous fit on the one hand forces Delano to dismiss his suspicions of the Spaniard but on the other once again leads him to articulate, in utter innocence, the very truth of the scene: "is it credible that I should have imagined he meant to spill all my blood, who can't endure the sight of one little drop of his own? . . . Well, well, he looks like a murderer, doesn't he? More like as if himself were to be done for" (p. 281). Their conversation about the peculiar voyage of the *San Dominick* resumes "between the intervals of shaving," as Babo keeps the razor at Cereno's neck in close check on his every word. Once more the suspicion occurs, prompted by something "hollow" in Don Benito's manner that seems reciprocated in Babo's "dusky comment of silence" that the two are "enacting this play of the barber," to "the very tremor of Don Benito's limbs," for some malign purpose. But "at last, regarding the notion as a whimsy, *insensibly suggested*, perhaps, by the theatrical aspect of Don Benito in his harlequin ensign, Captian Delano speedily banished it" (p. 282, my emphasis). The final image of the scene, here more clearly the narrator's than Delano's, depicts Babo as "a Nubian sculptor finishing off a white statue-head" and surveying "his master as, in toilet at least, the creature of his own tasteful hands" (pp. 282–83). Breaking more completely out of Delano's point of view into his own voice, the narrator himself articulates a metaphor that verges on the literal, and by merging the imminent decapitation of Don Benito with the artistry of Babo calls our attention both to the excruciating control of the slave turned master and to the perilous control that he himself has exercised, and continues to exercise, over the consciousness of the American captain.

The razor of Melville's narrative plays about the mind of Delano just as Babo's razor plays about the neck of Don Benito, regulating in a ritual of suppression the rebellion of recognition that threatens to occur at any moment. Reflecting at an earlier point upon the Spaniard's vexing questions about the American ship, questions delivered in "the manner of one making up his tale for evil purposes, as he goes," Delano decides that the design is too apparent, too bold, to be literally true, so that, as the narrator adds, "the same conduct, which, in this instance, had raised the alarm, served to dispel it" (pp. 262–63). This statement plays over every conceivable instance of Delano's suspicion and reaches a tormenting pitch in the shaving scene, where the boldly conducted ritual, made up for evil purposes by Babo as he goes along, both occasions and diffuses alarm. The scene's irony is held at razor's edge, the metaphoric at the absolute verge of becoming literal to such a degree that the tension can be rhetorically expressed only in a series of tautological statements that blindly bring Delano face to face with the literal and bring the narrator, dictating Delano's conduct as completely as Babo dictates Benito Cereno's, into virtual equivalence with the slave, both carrying out "plots" and expressing in mimic action their mutual authority through a suspended and agonizing ritual. Surrounding, containing, and rendering nearly irrelevant the conversation it encloses, the ritual articulates a terror that, as the Spaniard replies to one of Delano's inquiries about his ship's strange voyage, is indeed "'past all speech'" (p. 276).

III. THE CONTAGION OF SILENCE

"Benito Cereno," like "Bartleby" before it and *Billy Budd* after it, depicts the incipient and perilous merger of selves, the lawyer with Bartleby, Vere with Billy, and to a less evident extent, Delano with Benito Cereno. Bartleby's employer and Vere, in their fathoming of the mysterious regions of guilt to which they are exposed but for which they are not clearly culpable, become slowly enveloped in the tragedies of their titular characters, merging in sacrificial wastage with victims whose innocence and impenetrable passivity offer no handle for retort. The final tragedy of "Benito Cereno," in an irony verging upon tautology, depends on the fact that Delano in the end refuses or is unable to identify with Don Benito; but it is nonetheless the case that the mystery tale brings them into close approximation in a way that is all the more powerful in that it is virtually unconscious. We have noted that the "involuntary" character Freud ascribes to the process of joking defines it as a partially unconscious action and in conjunction with the naive, the humor of empty intention, that it thus clarifies the frustrating comedy which the interplay between Delano and the narrator produces. There is a further conjunction that defines the narrator's "dictation" of Delano's character in the fact that, just as the flawed signals presented to him promote "antic conceits" and trains of "involuntary suspicion" (p. 260) springing unconsciously into the narrative voice, so his response to Cereno in scenes which present no handle for retort often takes the form of unconscious or barely intended mimicry. He becomes at one point, for example, "involuntarily almost as rude" as Don Benito (p. 248); begins more and more to respond with coldness and reserve to the Spaniard's own apparently ill-bred reticence; is overcome by the "dreamy inquietude" and "morbid effect" of the mysterious calm (pp. 268, 272); and at extremity feels himself the victim of some sort of recurrent "ague" or "malady" that he strives to get rid of by "ignoring the symptoms" (pp. 273, 271). Cereno's "black vapors" (p. 263) seem slowly and surely to have infected Delano, bringing him involuntarily closer to the posture of the ruined captain and to the "disease" that the revolt, like the "contagious fever" of mutiny in *Billy Budd*, itself represents — a disease that many Americans in 1855 might well have tried to get rid of by ignoring the symptoms.

But since the narrative voice participates in Delano's malady, operating "insensibly" and "involuntarily" upon his otherwise "best regulated mind" and promoting suspicions and conceits that are both rebellious and feverishly contagious, we may see Delano's mimetic response to Don Benito's apparent "simulation of mortal disease" (p. 258) as a simulation in its own right, even in fact as a form of acting in *simile*, acting "as if," over which he has little control. The reflexive contagion that threatens Delano, like the contagion of revolt that has consumed the *San Dominick* and its sad captain, serves to bring the narrative yet closer to the breaking point of suppressed rebellion that the action of the tale contains; and like the brutally mimetic action of the shaving ritual, it defines an involuntary form of communication that at once merges and separates the captains by bringing them into a mirroring or tautological relationship, locked in a stance of communion and isolation. One important instance of ths relationship occurs just after Delano, the man "incapable of satire or irony," makes his unwitting remark to Cereno about the significant symbols of lock and key. Unable to shift the subject after the Spaniard drops into a swoon of withdrawal, Delano himself becomes "less talkative, oppressed, against his own will, by what seemed the secret vindictiveness of the morbidly sensitive Spaniard. But the good sailor . . . refrained, on his part, alike from the appearance as from the feeling of resentment, and if silent, was only so from contagion" (p. 257). The incipient merger of Delano and Don Benito is more disturbing than that of Bartleby and his employer, whose "sad fancyings — chimeras, doubtless, of a sick and silly brain — " lead him into tortured identification with the eccentric scrivener, precisely because Delano's receptivity to contagion is notably less conscious and because it is one that separates him from Cereno at the same time it unintentionally joins them in mimicked postures of reticence. The involuntary or unintentional character of the identification, like the empty intention of the naive, is crucial to the silent maintenance of suspense, just as Delano's simultaneous recognition and rejection in the shaving scene of a ritual that both is and is not, that is both literal and figurative, is crucial to the kind of merging and identification in language that defines the tautological suspense of the tale.

I spoke early on of the suspension of authorities that envelops the *San Dominick* as a form of mutual *abdication*, a silence or refusal to speak and act that both expresses and withholds authority by keeping it poised for possible implementation. In a tale whose concealed "plot" characteristically proceeds by "whispering" and the exchange of "silent signs" (p. 260), and in view of the derivation of *mystery* and *mystos*, from "silence" itself, Melville's own authorial abdication, like that of his characters, serves to form and define a moral riddle that deepens even as it is solved by fully participating in it. Like the "dusky comment of silence" that accompanies Babo's razoring, cunningly inserted between the talking and listening of the two captains, the silence that pervades Melville's tale in its atmostphere of suppressed articulation and failed communication is itself a form of expression that is "in between": between conversation, between each pair of the three captains, between ironies not completed, between the literal and the figurative, between the virtual tautology of what *is* and *is not* — between all these the razor of silence held in utter suspense. And between the reader and Delano the "unconscious" voice of the narrator engages in its silent, "involuntary" communications, at once abdicating and rendering its own authority by actively crossing what *Billy Budd* would designate "the deadly space between" and dictating, in an act of merger and separation, our own position between suspended possibilities. The irony or satire that Delano articulates but does not intend, we noted before, belongs more properly to the narrator, who in allowing neither captain a proper handle for retort to one another's failed communications, whether in word or gesture, maintains his own irony by constantly suppressing or silencing the rebellions against reason and regulation that Delano's "antic conceits" momentarily suggest, rebellions in which roles and identities begin to collapse and merge, and in which the conceit, the metaphoric, exists at the very edge of the literal.

The full character of Benito Cereno's ironic suspense and the ennervating power of its silence only come into proper perspective at the
end, however — not just the end of the mystery tale when in a "flash of
revelation" the true character of the revolt is revealed to Delano and the
skeletal figurehead of the *San Dominick* is exposed in completed irony,
but in the end of the entire tale, when the two captains, in the scene
given "retrospectively, and irregularly," stand once again in confrontation and the narrator proceeds to describe the spiritual wastage and
death of Don Benito and the "voiceless end" of Babo, his severed "head,
that hive of subtlety, fixed on a pole in the Plaza" (p. 315). The link between Babo as artist and Melville as narrator — both silently engaged in
the scheming of plots and the dictating of roles to their captains — that is
suggested in the shaving ritual is reenforced in this scene by the fact that
the narrator's exposition has itself been a "hive of subtlety" all along, and
moreover by the fact that the retrospective scene, in which Benito
Cereno articulates the haunting shadow of "the negro" that has descended
upon him, is itself a shadow that falls chronologically between the
mystery story of the revolt and the court proceedings that decisively
restore the threatened authority of the white masters. It is in this scene,
perhaps more properly than in Delano's moment of recognition, that
"past, present, and future [seem] one," for the retrospective act defines
once more in taut confrontation and projected wastage the moral dilemma that brings 1799 to verge perilously upon 1855 and merges the deca-
dent history of Spain with the now "slumbering volcano" (p. 262) of
America, the image of its heroic discoverer replaced by the skeleton of a
murdered slave-owner.

To guage the importance of this shadow, itself a "shadowy tableau"
that emerges from, but does not quite return to, the deep of the story
that produced it, it is necessary to note that the depositions, the most
elaborate ritual in a tale full of theater and ritual, act to suppress the
revolt and, in stately legal language, to reassert the precarious authority
of the "literal." Insofar as the depositions define the historical character
of Benito Cereno, who as Richard Harter Fogle notes, "is emerged with
the public occasion of his testimony, in the frame of his order," they do so
by the virtually silent dictation of indirect speech reproduced in
documents "selected, from among many others, for partial translation,"
but about which the suspicion arises in the tribunal that the deponent
"raved of some things which could never have happened" (pp. 299–300).
The flawed and cold-blooded depositions recount the rebellion selective-
ly and retrospectively, and in doing so they reenact and respond to an

escalating pressure to cure the disease aboard the *San Dominick*, restore regulation and order, and suppress the rebellion by legally *deposing* Babo. But as Edgar Dryden warns, the "factual additions" of the deposition may be "as unreal as the fictional world they burden," to such an extent, in fact, that "the juxtaposition of the fictional and the factual realms" destroys "the authenticity of each and leaves the reader face to face with a positive emptiness, an oppressive and threatening blankness" — a silent, "deadly space between."

It is on the authority of these markedly fragile and questionable documents that we are asked to reconstruct, in imagined memory, the mutiny that they formally suppress, and to distinguish between the voice of the tale, which engages in a rebellious creation of fiction, and the voice of the deposition, which apparently recites and reproduces the historical texts of the *actual* trial of the *actual* Captain Delano's *actual* account, from which the tale has, as it were, "involuntarily" sprung. The "fictitious story" dictated by Babo to Don Benito that the deposition alludes to but fails to reproduce (p. 307) thus points toward and in retrospect allies itself with the fiction of the mystery story created by Melville, itself suppressed and overturned by the stately, ceremonial, and "literal" language of the court. As a "key" that "fit[s] into the lock of the complications which precede it" (p. 313), the deposition ironically reverses these significant symbols, for while it explains the mystery, unlocks it, it also publically and legally locks up the significance of the revolt in chains and sentences that are incapable of satire and irony and as real as those that reenslave the revel slaves. As a return to what is legally literal, the deposition overthrows the suspended irony that momentarily makes master slave and slave master, undoes roles and scenes in which rebellious metaphors have themselves been dangerously close to becoming literal, and *retrospectively* suppresses the revolt of Melville's fictional version of Delano's history. And yet the final conversation of the tag ending, deferred by Melville and presented retrospectively, suggests that the authority of the deposition, riddled with lapses and obscured by "translation," is not complete, that in fact the hull of the *San Dominick*, "as a vault whose door has been flung back," does *not* lie completely "open to-day" (p. 313), but rather, like the enchanted deep, takes back what it gave while leaving a shadow of meaning suspended between.

Between the fiction and the history, the tale and the deposition, lies the shadowy confrontation of Delano and Benito Cereno, again joined and separated by their shared experience — on the one hand the American blind to Cereno's terror yet, like Vere in *Billy Budd*, acting in full and proper accord with the conventions that grant his authority; and on the other the Spaniard speaking the two haunted and haunting words, "the negro," after which there is "no more conversation" (p. 314). Were we to note the way in which lock and key form a figure for metaphor itself, a figure that fuses and isolates meaning in suspended confrontation, we might characterize the deposition and the tale, the history and the fiction, as parts of a metaphor, fused and separated in the act of merging their power while holding them in suspended distinction. Like the confrontation between Delano and Don Benito, the confrontation between the history and the fiction offers a virtual tautology, one that subsumes the various instances of tautology occurring throughout the tale and retrospectively exploits their charged potential. Such confrontations are not simply ironic, but by offering, as it were, no handle for retort to one another's enigmatic communications, they become dangerously equal. In between rebellion and suppression, or between the creation of authority and its exercise of mastery and decay into enslaving conventions, Melville seems to suggest, there lies the shadowed mystery of human suffering which conflicts in political action, as in the languages that grant those actions their perilous authority, contain and define — a mystery that like the wasted Benito Cereno and even more clearly like his slave and master, who "utter[s] no sound" and whose aspect seems to say, "since I cannot do deeds, I will not speak words" (p. 315), finally gives in to the flawed but explosive expression of its own silence.

Throughout the tale Melville himself cultivates the "icy though conscientious policy" of reserve that at one point leads Delano to characterize Don Benito as "a block, or rather . . . a loaded cannon, which, until there is call for thunder, has nothing to say" (p. 246). Only in the end does Melville, with neither the reticent cunning of the mystery story nor in the plagiarized cadences of his documents, speak in what seems his own voice. And yet as the finale to a tale in which he has permitted no burning off of his energies in philosophical speculation (as he does constantly in *Moby-Dick* and even in "Bartleby" and *Billy Budd*, for example) and in which the energy of psychological inquiry into character has been expended in the creation of physical scene and narrative response, the final tableaux are themselves strangely silent. Brief and hauntingly vivid, they continue to create the mystery rather than explain it, and they do so by revealing Melville's elected envelopment in the mystery's contagion of silence and his continued participation in the suspension of authority that animates the whole tale. Like Delano responding to the enigmatic Spaniard, Melville leaves "open margin" to his own "black-letter text" (p. 259). If the silent deaths of Benito Cereno and Babo comprise a marginal comment, they nonetheless conspire to make the asserted authority of the deposition more masterly and forceful. The deposition is no "empty" form, "artificially stiffened" like Don Benito's mock sword (p. 315); rather, it is the sword itself, the razor, perhaps, that descends upon the subtle hive of Babo's head.

The danger of equality, we noted before, is one to which Melville might well have been alive, not least because he was writing *Benito Cereno* on the eve of the Civil War in a climate of dramatic and explosive tension. That the story incorporates such tension, exploiting the myth of white innocence and creating in Babo a black every bit the equal of, and even the superior to, his masters, is painfully evident. What is more painful, more vexing and finally more powerful in Melville's tale is the degree to which it offers in suspended confrontation a choice between nearly tautological possibilities — between Delano and Cereno, between past and present, between history and fiction, suppression and revolt, or convention and creation — a choice in which their merger and isolation, in forms *separate but equal*, define the mechanisms by which societies are contained at the edge of rebellion and by which captains, peoples, and authors maintain and exercise their mastery.

M elville and the Slavery
of the North

Michael Paul Rogin

"Bartleby"

Early antislavery reformers, David Brion Davis has shown, rejected the slave master's lash in favor of impersonal, benign walls (in factories, and in the model prisons that would supersede the hangman's noose). "Instead of being whipped...and then set free with an unchanged heart," Davis explains, "the offender could now be placed behind walls...and transformed into a dependable and willing worker." Faced with the wall, the outcast would internalize self-discipline. The reformed vagabond, it was explained, would work from "neccessity of a moral kind, acting upon his rational nature; and from which brutal coercion differs as widely, as a nauseous drench in the mouth of an infant, from the medicated milk of its mother." "The slave-owner can whip his refractory slave to death," agrees Augustin St. Clair (in *Uncle Tom's Cabin*). But "the capitalist can starve him to death." The triumph of capitalism over chattel slavery meant not liberation for Melville, but the replacement of the whip by the wall.

The last whip which draws blood in Melville's fiction is the one with which [in *Pierre*] Glen Stanly brands Pierre. Whipping had justified murder in *White-Jacket,* and the only Melville protagonist actually to be whipped is Pierre. Pierre murders, and is jailed. Placed within the prison's "stone cheeks," he imbibes not "the medicated milk of [his]

From *Subversive Genealogy: The Politics and Art of Herman Melville.* © 1979, 1980, 1983 by Michael Paul Rogin. Knopf, 1983.

mother," but "death-milk" from Isabel. The walled interior is maternal, for Melville as for the reformers, but for him it is a tomb. "Bartleby" begins within the stone walls that crushed Pierre in the end.

Bartleby seemed a "dependable and willing worker," to recall David Brion Davis's words, in an office bounded by a "white wall" at one end and a "lofty brick wall" at the other. This "pallidly neat, pitiably respectable" young man, working at first with mechanical intensity, is a welcome contrast to the erratic scriveners his employer cannot control. "As if long famishing for something to copy, he seemed to gorge himself on my documents," the lawyer remembers. Deprivation seems to have reformed Bartleby; the documents are his medicated milk. He soon withdraws from legal copying into "dead-wall reveries," however, and his "passive resistance" gives him a mysterious hold on the lawyer. Bartleby extends, and drains of its excess, Isabel's passive power over Pierre. His story depicts the reform project of reclaiming Ishmaelites as one which twins the benefactor with his victim ["Bartleby" in *Billy Budd, Sailor and Other Stories*, ed. Harold Beaver (New York: Penguin Books, 1967) pp. 60, 66, 67, 78, 72; subsequent references in the text refer to this edition].

"How can the prisoner reach outside except by thrusting through the wall?" asks Ahab. "To me, the white whale is that wall, shoved near to me." Hemp finally strangled Ahab, but his project shattered against the leviathan's wall. Ahab's "white . . . wall" now imprisons Bartleby. Ahab's aggression, smashing against the wall through which the captain tried to strike, has turned inward. It presses relentlessly against the confined self.

Melville's [brother Gansevoort's] Jacksonian politics gave birth to Ahab. That democratic promise is a failure in "Bartleby." On Wall Street, politics is a mere patronage affair, servant of economic advancement. The lawyer has a political appointment, one of his employees is a machine politician, and Bartleby's fate gets confused with an election-day wager. Bartleby himself, it reassures the lawyer to think, lost his Dead Letter Office job "by a change in the administration" ("Bartleby," p. 99). A political change has also deprived the lawyer of his own patronage business. Jacksonian dreams offer meaning neither to Bartleby nor to his employer. Politics appears in the margins of this story. That failure of politics returns Melville to the fate of his brother.

"Bartleby" consigns the Wall Street lawyer to a Mastership in Chancery Court, the appointment from which Gansevoort Melville fled to political regeneration. Peter Gansevoort, soliciting letters which cited his nephew's "double revolutionary descent," obtained the chancery appointment for Gansevoort Melville. Gansevoort impressed upon his uncle the "vast importance of success in this matter to me." But Wall Street was hardly the arena in which a double descendant of revolutionaries could flower. If *Pierre* imagines what would have happened had Pierre Thomas Melvill returned to the Melvill house, "Bartleby" imagines Gansevoort Melville's fate had he never left his Mastership in Chancery.

"Bartleby" imagines that fate, however, not at the explosive apogee of Jacksonian politics, but after its exhaustion. Jacksonian democracy was the vehicle through which both Melville brothers had risen and fallen. Each had hoped to use it to throw off external models and speak in his own voice. "Bartleby" issues from the gloom of a writer whose project of liberation had failed, and who was now pressed to copy the models he had once repudiated. There was a scrivener who linked Gansevoort to Herman Melville. His name was James Ely Murdock Fly.

Fly was a friend of the Melville brothers. He was a classmate of Gansevoort's in the Albany Academy, and an apprentice lawyer and copyist in Peter Gansevoort's law office. Fly went west with Herman Melville in 1840 on the visit to Thomas Melvill. Then Gansevoort Melville supported his brother and Fly while they looked for work in New York. Both failed to obtain jobs, but when Melville shipped out on the *Achushnet,* Fly remained behind. He acted as intermediary between Peter Gansevoort and his nephew in the matter of the chancery appointment, and also sought Peter Gansevoort's help in securing a position as a Commissioner of Deeds. Melville's uncle told Fly to "doff your gown and slippers and step into the world of the metropolis" on his own. But Fly was not able to do so. A decade later he was with Melville in Pittsfield, for Melville had replaced Gansevoort as Fly's protector. His "old friend," he wrote Duyckinck, "has long been a confirmed invalid, and in some small things I act a little as his agent." When Melville cancelled his *Literary World* subscription after Duyckinck's chilly reception of *Moby-Dick*, he canceled Fly's, too. He made Fly the model for Pierre's devoted, ineffectual friend, Charlie Milthorpe. Fly died about the time Melville wrote "Bartleby." This shadow of a man — Bartleby to Gansevoort Melville's lawyer — was bequeathed by the failed political activist to his writer brother. Fly supplies the missing history of "Bartleby."

Melville deprives Bartleby of that history, however. "Confined within the limits of his own experience," as Georg Lukács says of the modern hero, Bartleby "is without personal history." Like the protagonist of a modernist fiction, he is existentially alone. "Beyond significant human relationship," in Lukács words, Bartleby is "unable to enter into relationships with other human beings." "He does not develop through contact with the world; he neither forms nor is formed by it." Bartleby inhabits, beneath tangible appearance, "the ghostly aspect of reality." Outside of history, he is given no specific social fate. Bartleby's absence of qualities, however, does place him historically. Bartleby inhabits the mass society that Tocqueville feared would triumph in America if meaningful, free, political action decayed. The power of Melville's short story comes from its abstractness. By resituating "Bartleby" historically, we can see it as comment on the historical triumph of abstraction.

The failure of political reform, alluded to in "Bartleby," confines the scrivener and his employer in the office they share. Economic relations replace political dreams. Unlike realistic fiction, however, "Bartleby" is not brought to life by a move from the spiritual to the concrete. It neither places egotistic man in the social complexity of rooted relationships, nor does it chart the breakdown of those relationships. It does allude to them, however. The lawyer's title, Master in Chancery, evokes the personal ties of dependence between master and apprentice. It recalls a time when apprentices, slowly learning the skills of their trade, looked forward to becoming masters in turn. Major Melvill, for example, had learned his trade as a merchant's clerk. When Allan Melvill and John Adams praised the passion for emulation as the source of personal achievement in America, they were speaking from a setting of masters and apprentices, of personal models and family connected avenues of mobility. Maria Melville, deploring her nephew Peter Gansevoort's lack of ambition, complained that he was "devoid of emulation, which urges so many on to exertion." Registering the shift from paternal models to maternal love, Maria blamed Mary Ann Gansevoort for her son's failure. But she, too, still inhabited a personal network of imitation and advancement. Melville's Master in Chancery, alluding to the traditional household organizaiton of work, underlines by contrast the anonymity of the modern office.

Bartleby's employer does not preside over apprentices, bound to him by learning a craft. He is master over a refractory slave, who first copies him "mechanically" (p. 67) and then withdraws his labor. Bartleby could imitate the lawyer forever without acquiring either his employer's competence or his status. The "degraded . . . drill" of the unskilled worker, the drill in which Bartleby engages, is "sealed off from experience; practice counts for nothing there." Bartleby's "I have given up copying" (p. 83) speaks to the changing character of work, the growing distance between master and employee, and the chasm separating imitation from maturity. Bartleby's jailer thought he was a "forger" (p. 99), appropriating another's identity through imitating his handwriting. Bartleby actually does the opposite. He appropriates the lawyer's identity by refusing to copy him. The lawyer recognizes the "wonderous ascendancy which the inscrutable scrivener had over me." How account for his "cadaverous triumph"? (p. 86).

Bartleby protests with "passive resistance" (p. 72), against his condition. In refusing to copy, he is copying Thoreau. "I simply wish to refuse allegiance," announced Thoreau, "to withdraw." Bartleby's "I prefer not to" is an echo of "Civil Disobedience." But just as Bartleby appropriates the lawyer to discredit him, so he undermines the Thoreauvian alternative. The intent of passive resistance was to save the adversary as well as to triumph over him. It avoided the costs of direct aggression. Richard Lebeaux suggests that Thoreau's father's weakness and his brother's death influenced Thoreau to choose a nonviolent form of rebellion. Melville had a weak, dead father and a dead brother, and he also stepped back from straightforward, aggressive triumphs. But "Bartleby" exposed the passive aggression which lies behind nonviolent resistance. Bartleby punishes the lawyer by punishing himself. He avoids a straightforward triumph, as Thoreau does, but in a way that inverts Thoreau's project. Bartleby undermines his adversary and destroys himself.

Already pale and "motionless" (p. 66) when he appears at the office, Bartleby successively detaches himself from each of his (already meager) social connections. He prefers not to read copy, prefers not to copy, prefers not to leave the office, haunts the office after the lawyer abandons it, and finally refuses to eat in jail. Turning aggression against himself, Bartleby refuses (by attacking the lawyer directly) to sanction the lawyer's anger at him. Bartleby exercises the power of weakness. The "young man" (p.66) taught obedience by the withdrawal of love (instead of by physical violence) is turning that lesson against this "elderly man" (p. 59).

Bartleby is formed solely from within the walls by which he is confined. Emptiness without means emptiness within. There is no transcendent flight from Wall Street routine either to nature or to the interior. Thoreau's speech embodies the feelings with which he resists appropriation. Bartleby's silence at once creates a wall between interior state and external appearance, and suggests that the former is merely a pale reflection of the latter. Thoreau "was not born to be forced"; Bartleby was. Nevertheless, by refusing to explain himself, he protects himself from colonization. Bartleby has the power of negativity. He drains his surroundings of the humanity in which the lawyer would like to believe.

Bartleby is Tocqueville's democratic individual, cut off from family, class, and community. He is "locked in the solitude of his own heart." He is the man, "himself alone," "not tied to time or place," that Tocqueville imagined as the subject of democratic art. Bartleby is alone not in nature, as Tocqueville predicted the hero of American poetry would be, but in the lonely crowd. Melville uses the paltry details of American life, which Tocqueville thought were artistically refractory, to make an aesthetic form.

The lawyer introduces his office by calling "spacious" the skylight shaft between his window and the white wall. "What landscape painters call 'life,' " he remarks, is visible through the opposing window, in the "lofty brick wall, black by age and everlasting shade; which wall required no spyglass to bring out its lurking beauties." No spyglass is needed because that wall "was pushed up to within ten feet of my window panes" (pp. 60 – 61). As the narrator finds life and variety in the view from his office, the words Melville puts into his mouth call that space a "cistern." The narrator's feeble, novelistic efforts, Melville is pointing out, are false to reality on Wall Street.

The lawyer's attempt to humanize his environment gives Bartleby his negative power. It is not so much the scrivener's withdrawal from life that needs explaining, as the way in which he draws in the narrator, the other employees, and the reader. The story hints at a social explanation for Bartleby's influence, and insists on a psychological one.

The routinization of work undermined the familially based set of master-apprentice relations. Employers and reformers claimed, in response, that their social institutions reproduced among strangers those shattered familial and communal bonds. As wage labor replaced household production, the employer insisted he was united to his workers by deeper ties than those of legal contract and market interest. Employers and their defenders spoke of workplaces as families. Reformers proposed asylums, modeled on the family, to reclaim the dangerous classes for useful work.

The office of a Master in Chancery was an appropriate place to test such claims. Chancery courts were centers of equity in the impersonal, rule-bound legal system. Peter Gansevoort presided over a chancery court in Albany; Gansevoort Melville did so in New York. As Master in Chancery, Bartleby's employer would have heard family disputes and settled contested wills. He might have disposed of the suit between Maria Melville and her brothers-in-law over Allan Melvill's debts to his father's estate. He might have heard the case between Mary Ann Gansevoort and her brothers-in-law over her share of Colonel Gansevoort's inheritance. Chancery courts merged legal proceedings with familial ties.

The chancery court was one arena for philanthropy; the Indian Office was another. Indians lacked the principle of emulation, Lewis Cass believed; his friend, Thomas McKenney, Commissioner of Indian Affairs, sought to instill it in them. McKenney adopted a young Choctaw, in the name of the American government, and brought him into the Office of Indian Trade. "The U. States Govt. are doing the part of a kind parent for him," McKenney explained; he employed the ward to copy his letters. The Indian rose by emulation to become a lawyer. Then, repudiating the path on which McKenney had set him, he returned to his tribe and represented it against the commissioner. The Choctaw lawyer was no more successful a rebel than Bartleby. His tribal connections were broken, and he could not forge new ties. Calling himself a "degraded outcast" from white society, he died, like Bartleby, a suicide.

McKenney was haunted by his ward's fate, just as Bartleby haunted the lawyer. The reason was the same: both reclamation projects required the consent of their targets. Bartleby acquires his power by withholding himself from the lawyer. The lawyer, like McKenney, is a philanthropist. He does not treat his employees by the counting-room calculus of the marketplace, firing them for their idiosyncratic inefficiencies. Nor does he subject them to the traditional coercive punishment once used against refactory workers. The lawyer does not discipline Turkey for his insolence. Attributing it instead to the copyist's ragged old coats, he gives Turkey a "respectable-looking coat" of his own (p. 64). It fails to calm Turkey's obstreperousness, however, and so the narrator welcomes the pallied young man who soon after appears at his door.

When Bartleby also proves difficult, the lawyer seeks to reach him with understanding. Like Theodore Parker, he does not want to treat this Ishmael "as Abraham his base-born boy," but rather help him find his "place on the wall." He tries, in turn, the various liberal strategies for overcoming the resistance of society's "dangerous" and "perishing classes." First he hopes that his benevolent paternalism will "purchase a delicious self-approval" (p. 72). That reform effort fails, as it generally did in Indian relations; it gives way (as in Indian policy) to cruder strategies. The lawyer tries to provoke Bartleby's active resistance, so he can justify aggression on his own. He tries to bribe him. He pretends that Bartleby does not exist. Finally he contemplates murder. But the lawyer draws back from these direct forms of aggression. Invoking Christ's injunction that "ye love one another" to stop himself from doing violence to Bartleby, he cites "self-interest" as a motive for "charity" (p. 88). The lawyer's interest is in preserving his self; for that purpose he needs to feel he has not done violence to Bartleby.

Thoreau voices the question Bartleby puts to the lawyer, "How shall he ever know well what he is and does as an officer of the government, or as a man, until he is obliged to consider whether he shall treat me . . . as a neighbor and well-disposed man, or as a maniac and disturber of the peace." Bartleby disturbs the lawyer's peace, but the lawyer tries not to treat him as a maniac. He wants to nurture Bartleby, but his charity reveals the failure of his office to sustain human life. At every step the lawyer takes toward Bartleby, Bartleby withdraws more deeply into himself. "Formerly tyranny used the clumsy weapons of chains and hangmen," wrote Tocqueville. "Despotism, to reach the soul, clumsily struck at the body, and the soul, escaping from such blows, rose gloriously above it; but in democratic republics . . . tyranny . . . leaves the body alone and goes straight for the soul." The lawyer "might give alms to [Bartleby's] body; but his body did not pain him; it was his soul that suffered, and his soul I could not reach." (p. 79).

Bartleby's withdrawals discredit the lawyer; they expose his bad faith. Unwilling to commit himself fully to the scrivener, he tries to set boundaries to the relationship. Those boundaries become Bartleby's targets. Contractual arrangements in the traditional workshop operated in a setting of tangible, specific, and customary reciprocal obligations. As persons and contracts separated, the bonds that would structure and limit Bartleby's expectations disappear. The lawyer needs to erect boundaries for Bartleby is boundaryless and insatiable.

The lawyer is nothing but his office, and he needs to have Bartleby in it. He experiences Bartleby as an "incubus" clinging to him (p. 90), but he cannot let him go. Their intimacy goes beneath that of paternal employer and prodigal son; it extends beyond class and ideology to personality. "Bartleby" is not just a parable of capitalist trying to reclaim worker, or father seeking forgiveness from son. Though set in the workplace, "Bartleby" offers the barest description of white-collar, working-class life. "Bartleby" is social critique not as realistic story but as psychological parable. It gains its power from the virtual disappearance of society, swallowed up in a psychological symbiosis. Bartleby (who has neither history nor speech) and the lawyer (who has neither name nor interior) are two halves of a single, divided self.

Folding doors divide the lawyer's office in two. His scriveners are on one side, and he is on the other. The lawyer palces Bartleby on his side of the folding doors, however, behind a screen and by a window facing a wall. The narrator is drawing "this quiet man" into his private space, and at the same time placing a division between them. He wants to "isolate Bartleby from my sight, though not remove him from my voice" (p. 67). He wants Bartleby to do his bidding without having to look at him face-to-face.

The lawyer is drawn to this "pitiably respectable, incurably forlorn" young man (p. 66). Bartleby seems at once needier and more tractable than his other scriveners. Because Bartleby has almost no self of his own, the lawyer thinks he can more easily absorb him. But the very absence of self, which allows Bartleby and the lawyer to merge, also introduces the withdrawal from life in which Bartleby will implicate the narrator. The symbiosis between Bartleby and his employer is a residue of that which twinned Isabel and Pierre. Pierre and the lawyer both engage in rescue operations to reclaim a lost interior. But the passion which seduces Pierre, because it is secretly present within him, is absent in the lawyer. Bartleby is the "ghost" (p. 90) left behind after the battle is over. He is the lawyer's interior, impoverished by a lifetime in contracts and deeds.

The lawyer is "an eminently *safe* man." He lives by avoiding risks; his "first grand point" is "prudence" (p. 60). "The lawyer's truth is not Truth, but . . . a consistent expediency," Thoreau protested. "His quality is not wisdom, but prudence." Thoreau was attacking Daniel Webster. He was calling for civil disobedience against the federal law that legalized slavery and made war on Mexico. Like Webster, Bartleby's lawyer stands "so completely within the institution" that he never distinctly and nakedly behold[s] it." The lawyer lacks heroic stature, or interior, personal authority. He is a "title-hunter" (p. 66) without a title of his own. He abdicates authority to the walls on the outside and to Bartleby within. Bartleby forces him to behold his instruction by withdrawing even further within it.

The lawyer's lack of authority makes him long for Bartleby's approval. To find a place of Bartleby would redeem his own impoverished life. The very internal emptiness which makes him fear Bartleby, however, makes him fear public opinion more. Rumors that Bartleby is "denying my authority" make him decide to evict the scrivener. "Buttoning up my coat to the last button," the lawyer emphasizes his physical separation from Bartleby. Still, he cannot "thrust him the poor, pale, passive mortal" away. "Rather would I let him live and die here, and then mason up his remains in the wall" (p. 90). [Social theorist] Theodore Parker had imagined that the outcast, once a "rejected stone," would find his "place on the wall, and his use." The lawyer would allow Bartleby his place, even if he had no use. In naming Parker's desire, however, the lawyer reveals it as a wish for death.

Public opinion forces the lawyer to abandon Bartleby; unwilling to use force and throw Bartleby out of his office, he "tore myself from him" instead (p. 92). The lawyer changes offices, but public opinion still connects him to the ghost that haunts his old quarters. "Fearful . . . of being exposed in the papers" (p. 93), he takes what seems the final step toward intimacy, and invites Bartleby home. Bartleby prefers not to go.

The lawyer hopes that "humanizing domestic associations" (p. 87) will nurture Bartleby. Bartleby prefers to underline the absence of those associations at work. The lawyer has fallen back on the separation of office from home; by making the office his home, Bartleby discredits that boundary too. Like Andrew Jackson, Bartleby retreats to his "hermitage" for privacy, to escape being "mobbed" in the metropolis (p. 81). But Bartleby's "hermitage," as the narrator calls it half a dozen times (pp. 69, 71, 74, 80, 88), is in his office; the lawyer's screen has located it there. Unlike the home in Nashville where Gansevoort Melville stayed, Bartleby's hermitage is no escape from society.

Finally, Bartleby is taken off to jail. There he might have joined Thomas Melvill, whose "sensibility" became "morbid," he wrote his brother, from being consigned to debtor's prison by his family. Bartleby was, as Thomas Melvill wrote, secluded "within these walls." His keeper might have been Leonard Gansevoort (Guert and Stanwix's father), who served as sheriff of Albany. He might have been confined by Peter Gansevoort, when he was Albany county court judge, or by Lemuel Shaw. Peter Gansevoort, who served as chairman of the committee on prisons in the New York state assembly, might have investigated Bartleby's condition. Lawyers, judges, and prison-keepers were everywhere in Melville's family. Melville, in negative identification, gained the capability of imagining a prisoner whom their authority could not reclaim.

"Under a government which imprisons men unjustly, the true place for a just man is also a prison," wrote Thoreau. Thoreau chose prison to declare his freedom from society. "I saw that, if there was a wall of stone between me and my townsmen, there was a still more difficult one to climb to break through before they could be as free as I was. I did not for a moment feel confined." Prison confirmed Thoreau's freedom; it confirms Bartleby's confinement. "Removed to the Tombs as a vagrant" (p. 95), Bartleby turns his face to the wall. "Look, there is the sky, and here is the grass," the lawyer tells him. "I know where I am," Bartleby replies (p. 96).

Bartleby is within the "walls of amazing thickness" that surround the prison yard. There the lawyer's wish to mason up his remains in a wall is fulfilled. The lawyer visits Bartleby one last time. He finds him "huddled at the base of the wall, his knees drawn up, and lying on his side." Assuming the foetal position, Bartleby has starved himself to death. The lawyer, however, finds rebirth even there. Within these "eternal pyramids," he observes, "through the clefts, grass-seed, dropped by birds, had sprung" (p. 98). Melville had imagined himself a seed, which had bloomed when it was taken from an Egyptian pyramid, and then fallen to mold. He puts Bartleby back to die within the Egyptian tomb. The seed dropped "through the clefts," like the "fertilizations" of Mount Greylock, does not generate human life.

As Thoreau imagined castles on the Rhine from within his prison cell, so Bartleby is "asleep . . . with kings and counselors" (p.99). The narrator's reference is to Job. "Why died I not from the womb?" cries Job. "Why did the knees prevent me? Or why the breasts that I should suck? For now . . . I should have slept: then had been at rest, with kings and counselors . . . as infants which never saw light." "There the prisoners rest together," Job thinks, " . . . which long for death." Job's outcry, with its references to knees and to refusing suck, describes the prisoner Bartleby. Bartleby has had Job's wish, and died in the womb. The lawyer's language betrays him to the end, however, for his invocation of Job undercuts his sentimentalizing of Bartleby's death.

The lawyer makes one last effort to circumscribe the meaning of his scrivener's fate. He reports the rumor that Bartleby was fired from the Dead Letter Office in Washington. It is too late to explain Bartleby away by his specific, historical origins. The formal economy and self-sufficiency of this story, by freeing the text from its historical referents, free Bartleby from his textual contines. He haunts the reader forever.

"The Paradise of Bachelors and the Tartarus of Maids"

The Atlantic Ocean separates copyists from lawyers in Melville's other sketch of working-class life, "The Paradise of Bachelors and the

Tartarus of Maids." The narrator of "The Paradise of Bachelors" participates in a dinner of English lawyers. "The Tartarus of Maids" narrates his visit to a factory whose work force is composed of virgins. Melville has moved the bachelor lawyer to London, and the pale mechanical worker to a Berkshire paper mill. This division deprives the story of "Bartleby"'s claustrophobic tension; nevertheless, "Paradise" and "Tartarus" are not two separate tales, but two halves of one.

Dining "not far from Temple Bar," the London lawyers are descended from the Templars. Lawyers interpret the holy writ of contractual society, as the Templars did in the medieval world. "The Templar is today a lawyer." The lawyers descend from the Templars, however, in the same sense that the cellar of Thomas Melvill's house, fictionalized in "Jimmy Rose," looked "like the ancient tomb of Templars." The cellar, like the lawyers' club and unlike the monastery, confines without regeneration. The religious faith and the military prowess of the Knights Templars gave them social power; the legalism of the bachelor lawyers cuts them off from the interior sources of the Knights Templars' authority. The lawyers in "Paradise" retreat from the world as do the Templars, but not in order to transform it. "[T]he dreamy Paradise of Bachelors, found in the stony heart of stunning London" is a refuge from family, from poverty, and from work [*Great Short Works of Herman Melville*, ed. Jerry Allen (New York, 1966), pp. 161, 163; subsequent references to "Bachelors" and "The Bell-Tower" in the text refer to this edition].

The lawyers replace systematic gloom with systematic gaiety; unlike the Wall Street lawyer, they have no scrivener in their lives. The "monk-knights" of the "sacred Brotherhood" of Templars ("Bachelors," p. 102) sacrificed sexuality to their calling; they gained worldly power in return. The captain of the *Bachelor*, in *Moby-Dick*, who has had great success hunting sperm whales, has acquired sperm oil. "Everything was filled with sperm, except the captain's pantaloon pockets, and those he reserved to thrust his hands into, in self-complacent testimony of his entire satisfaction." The *Bachelor*'s captain does not need the Polynesian girls dancing on his quarterdeck; hand in his sperm-free pockets, he satisfies himself. At the "Brethren of the Order of Celibacy," in London (p. 164), sex is sacrificed for food. The narrator reaches the Paradise of Bachelors from his hotel in Trafalgar Square. The parodic echo of Nelson ends at the dinner table, in a series of military metaphors. After the bachelors consume "the heavy artillery of the feast," then "like Blucher's army coming in at the death on the field of Waterloo, in marched a fresh detachment of bottles, dusty with their hurried march" (pp. 165–66). A "Jericho horn . . . with . . . two life-like goats' heads" is introduced at the end of the feast. The reference to Jericho portends retribution for the dinner-table pleasure; the goats' heads promise orgiastic consummation. But the horn is an emblem neither of judgment nor of Pan. The lawyer presiding at the table does not blow the horn. Instead, "our host . . . by his now inserting his thumb and forefinger into its mouth, . . . stirred up . . . the smell . . . of snuff" (p. 168).

"I suppose the Knights of the Round Table still assemble over their cigars and punch," Melville wrote Evert Duyckinck from Pittsfield. "I should like to hear again the old tinkle of glasses in your basement" in New York. Melville addressed Duyckinck from the family home at Arrowhead, cut off from urban, male conviviality. He was about to begin *Pierre*, his nightmare of family suffocation. The bachelor "band of brothers" (p. 167), by contrast, "had no wives or children to given an anxious thought." Paradise rescued urban bachelors from the family life of which Tartarus deprived rural maids.

Paradise and Tartarus are both places, like ideal families, outside the contaminating influence of society. Both are products of new forms of work, middle-class professionalism and working-class factory production, that separated labor from the household and thereby segregated the sexes. The cult of domesticity celebrated such segregation. "The Americans have applied to the sexes the great principle of political economy which now dominates industry," wrote Tocqueville. "They have carefully separated the functions of man and of woman so that the great work of society may be better performed. . . . You will never find American women in charge of the external relations of the family, managing a business or interfering in politics; but they are also never obliged to undertake rough laborer's work."

"The Paradise of Bachelors and the Tartarus of Maids" segregates the sexes to reverse their stereotypical occupations. The lawyers, unengaged in productive work, fail to leave their mark on the world. All they do is eat in Paradise, parodying consumption in the home. The daughters who had done household work on the farm now "undertake rough laborer's work" in the factory. Deprived of a domestic family circle, these celibate maids find their home in the mill.

The new mills appropriated both the women's work of household manufacture, and the women who engaged in it. As the factories drew work out of the home, their defenders justified them in familiar terms. Factories, it was said, replaced domestic paternal supervision. They would in-still in the mill girls "habits of order, regularity and industry, which lay a broad and deep foundation of public and private future usefullness."

That regularity was best achieved in the countryside. New England factory owners set their mills in nature, away from urban contamination. The owners benefited from cheap land and water power. The workers, absorbing nature's purity and subjected to factory discipline, benefited from pastoral harmony. The rural mills were virtuous, paternally governed communities, as their promoters presented them, adapting the republican order of the Puritans and the founders to an industrial age. The tradition which culminated in the mills and extended back to the early Massachusetts settlements was illustrated on the borders of the map of Pittsfield which Melville hung in his study. Jonathan Edwards's birthplace was depicted on one side of the map, a textile mill on the other. Both were set in nature; puritanism, industry and the land formed a harmonious whole.

Tartarus exploded that harmony. Melville made nature wild, and intensified mechanical discipline; the machine in the wilderness was beyond human control. The "monstrous shape" of the division of labor, wrote Marx, was "converting the workman into a living appendage of the machine." "We are regarded as living machines," the Lowell mill girls agreed. At Tartarus "the girls did not so much seem accessory wheels to the general machinery as mere cogs to the wheels" (p. 174).

"They took vows to serve their machines," wrote Michel Chevalier of the Lowell mill girls, " 'ere they had fully unfolded themselves." As Melville's bachelors were descended from the Knights Templars, the Lowell mill girls were, in John Greenleaf Whittier's words, the "fair unveiled Nuns of Industry." Protected by cloistered walls, "the nuns of Lowell," wrote Chevalier, "instead of working *sacred hearts*, spin and weave cotton." Melville remarked on the maids' devotional labors, too. He imagined the "pallid faces of all the pallid girls . . . dimly outlined on the imperfect paper, like the print of the tormented face on the handkerchief of Saint Veronica" (p. 180).

The factory, as such religious images indicate, was beginning to replace the church at the center of American life. The order and dedication seen in the mills was sanctified with religious associations. By borrowing the aura of the nunnery, apologists for the mills created an atmosphere of devotional chastity. Melville contaminated it. His barren mill girls are in the grip of a sexualized, mechanical power. The bachelors in Paradise and the Tartarus maids, separated from each other, remain virgins. Generative power is appropriated by the machine. Tartarus is not so much a family run by human authorities as a "whited sepulchre" (p. 170) dominated by its mechanical apparatus. The machine replaces God. It is the single, productive force in the double sketch.

"Where are the gay bachelors?" asks the visitor to Tartarus; then he sees "rows of blank-looking girls, with blank, white folders in their blank hands, all blankly folding paper." One pale girl stands at a "huge frame of ponderous iron, with a vertical thing like a piston periodically rising and falling" (p. 174). There are "rows of girls" upstairs, each "haltered" to "a long glittering scythe" (p. 176). The rags shredded against the scythes, mixed with the red water from "Blood River," turn into "white pulp." In "nine minutes," "a scissory sound smote my ear, as of some cord being snapped," and the machine delivers blank white sheets of paper (pp. 177–79). Tartarus stands in a valley, at the bottom of "Black Notch" (p. 168). The extended sexual metaphor—of crotch, phallus, "germinous particles" of semen, vagina dentata, umbilical cord, and birth—is deliberate and unmistakable.

The Swedish writer Fredrika Bremer visited the Lowell mills on her trip around America. The travel volume she published shortly before Melville wrote "Tartarus" depicted "young girls standing—each one between four busily-working spinning jennies . . . and guiding them much as a mother would watch over and tend her children. The machinery was like an obedient child under the eye of an intelligent mother." Bremer imposed the cult of domesticity on the factory; Melville inverted it. At Tartarus the maids are obedient children, bound to a throbbing machine. Bremer's mothers tending the child-machine become passive children. Her "obedient child" machine acquires, in Tartarus, monsterous, sexual, maternal power.

The narrator watching the manufacture of paper thinks of "John Locke, who, in demonstration of his theory that men had no innate ideas, compared the human mind at birth to a blank sheet of paper" (p. 179). The blank sheets born at Tartarus, however, bear the invisible stain of human labor. Their whiteness calls attention, by what is erased on Locke's tabula rasa, to the labor both of production and of reproduction. Mechanical production does not replace human labor; it takes it over. The sexualization of the machine contrasts with the white-faced humans reduced to sterility.

The visitor to Tartarus is a "seedsman," and a boy named Cupid guides him through the mill (pp. 170, 177). He imagines to Cupid that "Among these heaps of rags, there may be some old shirts, gathered from the shirts of dormitories of the Paradise of Bachelors. But the buttons are all dropped off." Cupid confuses these "bachelors' buttons" with "the *flowers* . . . the Bachelor's Buttons . . . Or did you mean the gold bosom-buttons of our boss, Old Bach?" (p. 176). A seedsman without seed, bachelors' buttons without buttonholes, flowers that don't bloom, and a bachelor supervisor of Tartarus maids all compose an extended image of barrenness.

That image contrasts with the generative boasts of those celebrating the new factories. Nature was sterile without the fructifying hand of man, said Edward Everett at Lowell. The absense of industry, Everett warned, reduced "nature's grand and lovely landscape gardening of vale and mountain" to a "dull alluvial level." "It is the contrast of production with barrenness; of cultivation with waste." Melville brought that contrast into the mill. The mechanical cultivation of nature, in his sketch, sterilized Tartarus maids.

"Lowell is the garden of Eden (except the serpent)," the Lowell *Editorial* announced. "The tree of the knowledge of good is there, but the evil is avoided through the judicious management of the superintendent." Melville's superintendent protects his virgins not in Eden but in Tartarus. "The Tartarus of Maids," to be sure, depicts factory life with no more realistic, surface detail than that offered by the Lowell *Editorial*. As in "Bartleby," however, variety and detail are sacrificed to reach a deeper truth. The brick buildings across the Hudson River, whitewashed to look like marble, at first fooled Tocqueville; they presented a false front to the world. Painted surfaces would, in the same way, obscure the "whitewashed . . . white sepulchre" at Tartarus (p. 170). Paint would cover over the charnel house within. Like a photographic negative, "Tartarus" drains the local color out of the mill.

Factory promoters distributed a picture of Lowell mill girls peacefully tending their machines. Looked at with Melvile's eyes, the identical young women in identical rows resemble automatons. These are not the women workers who wrote letters and verse, and organized to protest their regimentation. Melville ignores such autonomous subjects, who gained individual voices in the course of their collective struggle. Melville offers a fable instead, which turns the philanthropic dream of social order against its dreamers.

Defenders of industrial capitalism not only harmonized workers with machines, they also replaced workers by machines. "Labor is the source of wealth," insisted Daniel Webster, but he rejected the view that, distinguishing labor from capital, regarded as labor mainly "the toil of the human arm." Webster included "the labor of the ox, and the horse," and the machine. His view of labor merged together human, animal, and mechanical power. It obliterated the human labor Locke had placed at the source of production; Webster's machines had no humans attached to them at all. The Squire of Marshfield acknowledged workers, to be sure, but his laborers made money and rose into the middle class; they did not work. "Carolina cotton is carried to the County of Berkshire," he exulted (naming the county where Melville lived), "and . . . labor in Berkshire is . . . higher than it was ever known before." How, then, asked Webster, could labor be in conflict with machine-utilizing capital? "It would be quite as reasonable to insist, that the weaving of paper . . . in consequence of recent most valuable mechanical inventions, should be suppressed." The weaving of paper at Tartarus exposed the work process hidden beneath Webster's panegyric.

Webster went further. The humans he repressed in the process of production returned in his humanized machines. "Mechanic inventions," he explained, are not "labor-saving machines," but "labor-doing machines; because they in fact are laborers." While the human worker needed to eat, his fellow-laboring machine did not. Bartleby, who gorged himself on documents, also lived without dining. The Tartarus maids, particularly in contrast to the bachelor gourmandizers, seem to do so as well. Melville's workers, drained of their life by mechanical processes, do not eat. Webster's workers ate, but they could be replaced by machines. He explained,

> The world is precisely as much benefited as if Providence had provided for our use millions of men, like ourselves in external appearance, who would work and labor and toil, and who yet required for their subsistence neither shelter, nor food, nor clothing. These automata in the factories and the workshops are as much our fellow laborers, as if they were automata wrought by some Maelzel into the form of men, and made capable of walking, moving, and working, of felling the forest or cultivating the fields.

"The Bell-Tower"

Melville fictionalized a figure like Maelzel as the Renaissance inventor, Bannadonna, in "The Bell-Tower." "Stocking the earth with a new serf, more useful than the ox," Bannadonna wrought an automaton into the form of a man. His serf was the "iron slave," Talus. The "practical mechanics" Webster celebrated found its champion in the "practical materialist," Bannadonna.

Bannadonna built a mechanical clock. He represented each hour by a female figure; Talus was to emerge at sixty-minute intervals and strike the hour. Webster's rhetoric made human laborers disappear; Bannadonna kills an artisan whose timidity during the casting of the giant bell threatens to spoil his creation. The worker disappears into the boiling vat. Seeking (like his prototype, Victor Frankenstein) the triumph of technology over biology, Bannadonna sacrifices a human worker to his living machine. And he invents a slave that will strike the figures of women twenty-four times a day.

Pierre worshipped at the "one-pillared temple" to his father. The "unblest foundling, Bannadonna" ("Bell-Tower," p. 197), builds his "central pillar" himself. He erects a church bell-tower, and places his clock upon it. This "tower was titanic." "Mounting it, he stood, erect, alone" above the Alps (as Pierre could not do in the Berkshires), celebrating his power over nature (p. 198).

The clock on the bell-tower blessed a new religion, that of material invention. It announced the regulation of industrial work, not by the rhythms of nature, biology, and the workers' traditional or self-chosen pace, but by the routine of mechanical time. Nineteenth-century factory bells performed that regulatory function. They governed workers' lives like clockwork. "Go listen to the slavish bell that turns an Eden into hell," rhymed a Lowell labor-reform paper. Bannadonna keeps his slave hidden until the first, ceremonial ringing of the bell. When Talus struck the first hour, Una, he would announce the new invention to the town. Una was the name of Hawthorne's daughter. The mark on the face of the clock figure (caused when Bannadonna pushed his worker into the cauldron) echoes Hawthorne's "The Birthmark." Hawthorne's Aylmer sought to make his wife perfect by extracting her birthmark, and killed her. As Bannadonna becomes absorbed in contemplating Una's blemish, the "no more becloaked Talus" strikes the hour and kills his master (p. 206). Bannadonna leaves no monument behind, moreover, for the giant bell-clock proves "too ponderous for its frame." As its bells toll Bannadonna's funeral, "the groined belfry crushed sideways in" (p. 212). Unable to suport the weight of its bells, the collapsing phallus falls to the ground.

Bannadonna conceived his project by watching the bellringers stationed aloft in the belfry. A figure viewed from such a distance, writes Melville, "evinces no personality. Instead of bespeaking volition, its gestures rather resemble the automatic ones of the arms of a telegraph." The human figure thus beheld has a "purely Punchinello aspect," and Bannadonna determines to "devise some mechanical agent" in imitation (p. 208). Melville is describing not only Bannadonna's project but his own. "Bartleby," "Paradise," "Tartarus," and "The Bell-Tower" all reduce human figures to marionettes without personalities. This distancing, mechanizing effect gives *Bartleby* its hypnotic power, but it weakens the other two sketches. They suffer from their allegorical quality. Both allude to a living true religion in the past—Catholicism in "Paradise," Hebraism in "The Bell-Tower." Both contrast that faith to a slavish, mechanical order. The contrast is too easy, and it deprives the sketches of life. In one tale, however, Melville brilliantly combines reference to past religion with the replacement of personalities by marionettes. Between "Tartarus" and "The Bell-Tower," he wrote "Benito Cereno." The three tales, written one right after the other, connect chattel slavery with enslavement to machines.

Radical abolitionists made the same connection. "The laboring man," wrote Thoreau, "has no time to be anything but a machine." "I sometimes wonder that we can be so frivolous," he complained, "as to attend to the gross but somewhat foreign form of servitude called Negro Slavery, there are so many keen and subtle masters that enslave both north and south." "Visit the Navy Yard," he suggested. There you will see "such a man as an American government can make . . . with its black arts." If it is a question of merely obeying directives, "wooden men can perhaps be manufactured that will serve the purpose as well."

Bannadonna manufactures such a man, and Melville calls Talus a slave. Most Northerners, however, contrasted Southern slavery to the Northern use of machines. "The work of machinery is certainly labor in all senses, as much as slave service," Webster admitted. The difference was that Southern servitude enslaved humans to create value, and Northern technology did not. The steam engine would be "our artificial slave," Elizur Wright promised; the industrializing North needed no human chattel. "No overseer ever dared use the whip" over Northern workers, a labor reformer agreed, but the factory operative was a "poor slave" nonetheless. "A slave['s] . . . will is . . . quickened by the whip of the overseer. The whip which brings us to Lowell is NECESSITY." At Tartarus "machinery—that vaunted slave of humanity—here stood menially served by human beings, who served mutely and cringingly as the slave serves the Sultan" (p. 174). Striking Lowell workers sang, to the tune of "I Won't Be a Nun," "I'm so fond of liberty I cannot be a slave."

Melville, however, found no rebellion at Tartarus. His maids are passive; the figure that revolts is the "iron slave to Bannadonna." The epigraph introducing "The Bell-Tower" announces, "Like negroes, these powers own men sullenly; mindful of their higher master; while serving, plot revenge" (p. 195).

Witches and Wall Street: Possession Is Nine-Tenths of the Law

Michael Clark

I would like to begin by reading two different dialogues. The first is from Cotton Mather's *The Wonders of the Invisible World* (Boston, 1693), an account of the witchcraft trials held in Salem in 1692. It is a section from the examination of Susannah Martin. The second dialogue is from Melville's "Bartleby the Scrivener" (first published in *Putnam's Monthly Magazine* in 1853 and reprinted in *Billy Budd and Other Tales* [New York: Signet Classics, 1961], pp. 122–23; all page numbers refer to this edition).

> MAGISTRATE: Pray, what ails these People [who have been
>   brought to testify against you]?
> MARTIN: I don't know.
> MAGISTRATE: But what do you think ails them?
> MARTIN: I don't desire to spend my judgment upon it.
> MAG: Don't you think they are bewitch'd?
> MAR: No, I do not think they are.
> MAG: Tell us your Thoughts about them.
> MAR: No, my thoughts are my own, when they are in, but
>   when they are out they are another's. Their Master—
> MAG: Their Master? who do you think is their Master?
> MAR: If they be dealing in the Black Art, you
>   may know as well as I.
> MAG: Well, what have you done towards this?

From *Texas Studies in Literature and Language* 25, no. 1 (Spring 1983). © 1983 by the University of Texas Press.

MAR: Nothing at all.
MAG: Why, 'tis you or your Appearance.
MAR: I cannot help it.

> "Bartleby," said I, gently calling to him behind his screen. No reply.
>
> "Bartleby," said I, in a still gentler tone, "come here; I am not going to ask you to do anything you would prefer not to do—I simply wish to speak to you."
>
> Upon this he noiselessly slid into view.
>
> "Will you tell me, Bartleby, where you were born?"
>
> "I would prefer not to."
>
> "Will you tell me anything about yourself?"
>
> "I would prefer not to."
>
> "But what reasonable objection can you have to speak to me? I feel friendly towards you...."
>
> "What is your answer, Bartleby?" said I, after waiting a considerable time for a reply....
>
> "At present I prefer to give no answer," he said, and retired into his hermitage.

These two passages bear an obvious resemblance to one another. They are both juridical interrogations: literally in Susannah Martin's case and stylistically in Bartleby's, whether or not the narrator knows he is using the discourse of his profession. Moreover, both Bartleby and Martin defend themselves from the questions with the same rhetorical gesture. His "I would prefer not to" clearly echoes her "I do not desire to spend my Judgment upon it," and her laconic refusal to give her judges anything they can construe as evidence—"My thoughts are my own, when they are in, but when they are out they are anothers"—eloquently articulates the strategy by which Bartleby eludes the earnest goodwill of the narrator.

There are, of course, more obvious differences between the dialogues, even if for the moment we disregard the fact that Melville's tale is fiction and Susannah Martin's story terribly real. Bartleby has no apparent reason for resisting the narrator's efforts to find out about him, whereas Martin knew that her life depended on her answers. Similarly, the magistrates who questioned Martin were trying to establish evidence that she had pledged herself to the Devil, whereas the motives behind the narrator's questions are plainly less malevolent. What I want to suggest, however, is that these differences are less significant than the parallels between the epistemological assumptions and strategic ends that underlie the exchanges. In short, I believe that the narrator and the examiners use the same methods to explain deviant behavior and that they intend that explanation as a means of control. The examiners' success indicates the profound conjunction between this strategy and the grounds of social order in the Puritan community; the narrator's failure suggests that his is a Puritan mind caught in an un-Puritan world.

When Susannah Martin stood before the court at Salem, a great deal more was at stake than her life. As Cotton Mather explained in a sermon included in *Wonders*, the ontological barriers between the visible world of man and the invisible world of the spirit were not crossed easily. The manifestation of any spiritual activity in the corporeal world was therefore a direct indication of God's special providence: "not a Devil in the Air, can come down without the leave of God," Mather said, and he went on to explain that such an extraordinary dispensation could be motivated by only two conditions: a divine judgment of man's guilt and the Second Coming:

> There is a Court somewhere kept; a Court of Spirits, where the Devil enters all sorts of Complaints against us all. . . . If our Advocate in the Heavens does not now take off his Libels; the Devil, then, with a Concession of God, comes down, as a destroyer upon us.

> I am suspicious, that there will . . . be an unusual Range of the Devil among us, a little before the Second Coming of our Lord. . . . The devil is going to be dislodged of the Air, where his present Quarters are; god will with flashes of hot lightning upon him cause him to fall as lightning from his ancient habitations. . . . Now a little before this thing, you be like to see the devil more sensible and visibly busy upon earth perhaps, than ever before.

The question of Susannah Martin's guilt, then, was not simply a matter between her and God. Her God was the God of New England as well, and if the various offenses charged against her (some drowned oxen, a dead cow, etc.) could be attributed to the work of the spirits, then there was a distinct possibility that the Last Judgment was at hand.

The immensity of these implications helps explain why the people of New England zealously persecuted witches after England and Europe had lost interest in them. For the Puritans a close examination of the misfortunes that plagued them could determine the state of their own spiritual condition and, even more important, could situate New England within the typological history which was leading them all to judgment. Within this context the physical and psychological torment to which they subjected their neighbors, friends, and sometimes members of their own families was nothing other than a desperate hermeneutic practiced at the edge of time.

Part of the urgency infusing the witchcraft trials derived from the difficulty of their hermeneutic task. The judges could not directly determine whether or not an evil spirit was at work in some extraordinary event because spirits are confined to the invisible world. In one of his frequent pleas for caution and mercy, Matner warned, "But what shall be done, as to those against whom the evidence is chiefly founded in the dark world? Here they do solemnly demand our Addresses to the Father of Lights, on their behalf. But in the mean time, the Devil improves the Darkness of this Affair, to push us into a Blind Mans Buffet, and we are even ready to be sinfully, yea, hotly, and madly, mauling one another in the dark."

The judges were therefore extremely reluctant to make the connection between material events and such evidence as existed only in the invisible world. This reluctance is reflected in Mather's own caution about using natural phenomena to support his suspicion that the Second Coming is near. "The usual Walls of defence about mankind have such a Gap made in them," Mather says, "that the very Devils are broke in upon us . . . as if the Invisible World were becoming Incarnate." "Now at last," he remarks in the same address, "the Devils are (if I may so speak) in person come down upon us." When Mather does drop these qualifications, it is at the rhetorical climax of his jeremiad, and he clearly recognizes that he is violating not only his own insistence on the metaphorical nature of spiritual explanations but that of the audience as well: "Behold, Sinners, behold and wonder, lest you perish: the very Devils are walking about our Streets, with lengthened Chains, making a dreadful Noise in our Ears, and Brimstone, even without a Metaphor, is making a hellish and horrid stench in our Nostrils."

Clearly, Mather was willing to sacrifice orthodoxy for impact at such moments. When he uses natural evidence in the course of a systematic theological argument, however, his procedure is quite different. In the sermon contained in *Wonders*, Mather eschews coy disclaimers and rhetorical hyperbole and instead carefully situates the hermeneutic use of the events within providential time. Borrowing from Puritan traditions of scriptural exegesis in the following passage, Mather carefully distinguishes between natural and supernatural causes for extraordinary events, and he makes the connections between the visible and invisible worlds contingent upon the place of those events in relation to the Second Coming. Until then, Mather says, the relationship between cause and event simply points to the ultimate union of the visible and invisible through analogy:

> One Woe that may be look'd for is, a frequent Repetition of Earth-quakes, and this perhaps by the energy of the Devil in the Earth. The Devil will be clap't up, as a Prisoner in or near the Bowels of the earth, when once that Conflagration shall be dispatched, which will make, The New Earth wherein shall Dwell Righteousness; and that Conflagration will doubtless be much promoted, by the Subterraneous Fires, which are a cause of the Earthquakes in our Days.

This eschatological hermeneutic is, of course, very similar to typological interpretation, with the important exception that the two "events" being compared here are not exactly historical parallels. They are two different pairs of event and cause, and they differ only in the hermeneutic method that establishes the connection between the event and its cause. In other words, an earthquake may be explained by natural causality, or it may be explained metaphysically. The adequacy of one method or the other is determined by — and so indicates — our place in time in relation to the Last Judgment.

A similar, though less precise, attitude governed the evaluation of evidence at the trials. The direct demonstration of spiritual possession in the form of visible spirits was quite rare. It was called "spectral evidence" and was usually discredited because only the possessed could see spirits. The presence of spirits could therefore be discovered only indirectly through the hermeneutic determination of the invisible causes of visible events. Two kinds of evidence exemplify this principle. One of the most common occurrences at witchcraft trials was the victims' sudden seizures by fits which prevented them from giving their testimony. Mather describes the case of Elizabeth Pacy, who upon being brought before the witch that tormented her "was made utterly senseless, during all the time of the Trial: or at least speechless." This problem was usually cured by one of several methods: the husbands or parents of the possessed victims made the accusation for them; the court was forced "with much Patience to obtain, by much waiting and watching" the testimony directly from the victims (often with considerable "advice" about what should be said); or, as in Deodat Lawson's account of the New England trials, a scriptural text was read against the evil spirit:

> [the victim] seemed to dispute with the Apparition about a particular Text of Scripture. The Apparition seemed to deny it; (the woman's Eyes being fast closed all this time) she said, She was sure there was such a Text, and she would tell it; and then the Shape would be gone, for, said she, I am sure you cannot stand before that Text: Then she was sorely Afflicted . . . And then said, I *will* tell, I *will* tell; it is, it is, it is, three or four times, and then was afflicted to hinder her from telling, at last she broke forth, and said, It is the third Chapter of the Revelations. . . . I began to read, and before I had near read through the first Verse, she opened her Eyes, and was well.

Another kind of evidence that was frequently cited in witchcraft trials was the presence of strange growths or sores on the body of the victims. At the trial of Martha Carrier in Salem, Mather says, Benjamin Abbot testified that after he had argued with Carrier one day a sore appeared in his groin. It was lanced by a doctor, but another sore immediately appeared. "He was brought unto Death's Door," Mather tells us, "and so remained until Carrier was taken, and carried away by the Constable, from which very day he began to mend, and so grew better every Day, and is well ever since."

Both kinds of evidence could prove that a witch was tormenting the victim, and for the same reason. The judges argued that if an arrest cured the sore when medical treatment had failed, the cause of the sore could not have been natural and therefore must have been spiritual. Similarly, any illness that could be cured by reading a biblical text must have been caused by a malevolent spirit rather than any natural disease, since there is no visible or natural connection between Scripture and the body. This reasoning clearly follows Mather's proposition that natural events may have either a natural or spiritual cause. But Mather, you will remember, was able to choose between the natural and spiritual causes only by interpreting the event from the perspective of providential time or a divine judgment about the state of man's spiritual condition. That perspective was available to him only through an analogical projection or, more generally, as a metaphor based on the natural causality that he *could* clearly demonstrate. Not even Cotton Mather was willing to declare that he could speak from the divine perspective which would make spiritual causality certain. The judges, on the other hand, were faced with a pressing practical problem: they, too, were limited to human time and corporeal vision but had to make a decision that left no room for parenthetical disclaimers and that determined the defendant's life.

The solution to the magistrates' dilemma lay in the way evidence was gathered. In the cases I have described, the event was proven *not* to be derived from a natural cause by the intervention of an agent associated with social order and authority: ministers, magistrates, constables, and — I insist on this parallel — parents and husbands. In each case this intervention occluded natural causality and so discovered the connection between the event and a spiritual cause. The arrest of Martha Carrier, for example, proves that the sore responds to legal action rather than medical, which allows the interpretation of the sore as a spiritual phenomenon. The connection between power and the exegetical function is even more evident in the case of husbands and magistrates, since they often literally put words in the mouths of their social inferiors in order to prove the presence of spirits.

In the witchcraft trials, then, authority performs the same hermeneutic function that interpretation performs for Mather: it drives a wedge between the event and its natural cause and so allows a connection between the event and a spiritual cause. In Mather's sermon the knowledge of that connection issues from the metaphorical projection of the providential perspective. In the trials that knowledge was constituted'not by providence but by power, the very channels of social hierarchy through which evidence emerged. In short, for the New England Puritans in 1692, power was knowledge. To rule was to know, and it was through knowledge that power was exercised. No wonder Susannah Martin would not tell the magistrates what she thought. Her refusal, of course, did no good:

> MAG: What is the reason these [witnesses] cannot come near you?
>
> MAR: I cannot tell it may be the Devil bears me more malice than another.
>
> MAG: Do you not see God evidently discovering you?
>
> MAR: No, not a bit for that.
>
> MAG: All the congregation besides think so.
>
> MAR: Let them think what they will.

They did, and two months later she was hanged.

By the time "Bartleby the Scrivener" appeared in 1853, the witch-craft trials had become a historical relic, the object of sensational curiosi-ty, some vague ancestral guilt, and, more frequently, a bemused tolerance for the idiosyncrasy of an age gone by. Three years before Melville's story was published, Nathaniel Hawthorne had embodied most of these attitudes in *The Scarlet Letter*, where the "Witch-lady" Mistress Hibbins confronts Hester and Pearl with a "hist, hist," her "ill-omened physiognomy" hanging above them like the villain from a fairy tale. Like most "Puritans" in the novel, she is little more than a piece of the narrative machinery. The quick, caricatural strokes in which she is sketched are as different from the rich lines of Hester as Pearl's am-biguous petulance is different from the stilted gestures of the little Puritans who torment her with cries that evoke the pastness of their set-ting rather than the cruelty of childish malice: as Hester and Pearl ap-proach them, "the children of the Puritans looked up from their play, — or what passed for play with those sombre little urchins, — spake gravely one to another: — 'Behold, verily, there is the woman of the scarlet letter; and, of a truth, moreover, there is the likeness of the scarlet letter running along by her side! Come, therefore, and let us fling mud at them!' "

Obviously, historical realism is not the point of such passages. Hawthorne could render seventeenth-century New Englanders more credibly than this, as "The Gentle Boy" and "Young Goodman Brown" attest. In *The Scarlet Letter*, however, Hawthorne has reduced his Puritans to a collection of stereotypes, and they function in the novel as a narrative shorthand, a concise set of gestures, costumes, and archaisms which form the background against which the complex psychological drama of the novel is set. Much of the novel's affective power comes from the conflict between Hester's and Dimmesdale's exquisite sensitivi-ty and the unbending moralism of the characters around them, and when Hawthorne does utilize his subtle and profound understanding of the Puritan culture and character — as in the episode in the Governor's Hall or in the varied response to the appearance of the comet in chapter 12 — his end is not historical accuracy so much as it is deliberate nar-rative ambiguity. This opposition of historical and narrative uses of Puritanism is even more dramatic in "Alice Doane's Appeal," where Hawthorne's narrator takes the two young girls accompanying him to the very hill on which the Salem witches were executed in order to "court the historic influence of the spot" and, one suspects, his young companions as well. But on Gallows Hill, now covered with a plentiful crop of dark, glossy woodwax, all traces of the executions have vanished; and despite the "feminine susceptibility" of his companions, only the narrator is sensitive to the melancholy associations he feels must surround the hill. So instead of trying to call up the spirits from beneath their feet, the narrator pulls out a manuscript that he happens to have in his pocket and begins to read "a wondrous tale of those old times" complete with young lovers, a stormy night, and a full complement of ghosts. This works. Before he can finish, "my companions seized an arm on each side; their nerves were trembling; and, sweeter victory still, I had reached the seldom trodden places of their hearts, and found the well-spring of their tears. And now the past had done all it could."

In such examples Puritanism clearly appears as a particular turn of mind rather than a historical fact, a way of looking at the world rather than a way the world ever was. Melville used the Puritan past in the same way, despite his more self-consciously philosophical treatment of theological themes. His work is pervaded by discussions of hubris, guilt and innocence, predestination, and faith; and in works such as *Moby-Dick* and *The Confidence-Man*, crucial turns of the plot hinge on dramatizations of such abstract issues as theories of scriptural hermeneutics and the intelligibility of natural signs. These concerns are relevant to most religions, of course, but at least in the 1850s, Melville thought of the obsessive concern with the invisible significance of visible things as specifically Puritan. In his review of Hawthorne's *Mosses from an Old Manse*, for example, Melville speculates that the "other side" of Hawthorne's soul, the "mystical darkness" setting off the lighter side of his work, may be the result of a "touch of Puritanic gloom" that drives him beneath the bright surface of life to explore its hidden secrets. And inspired perhaps by the republication of Cotton Mather's *Magnalia Christi Americana*, also in 1853, the narrator of "The Lightning-Rod Man" casts out "that dark lightning-king" and his "tri-forked thing" with words that would have sounded entirely appropriate at the lips of a Puritan minister: "I stand at ease in the hands of my God. False negotiation, away! See, the scroll of the storm is rolled back; the house is unharmed; and in the blue heavens I read in the rainbow that the Deity will not, of purpose, make war on man's earth."

To the sophisticated reader of 1854, the battle between the enthusiastic lightning-rod salesman and the narrator of that story, fought in a remote cottage on a dark and stormy night, must have seemed like a nostalgic reflection on the struggle to replace superstition with science, a schoolboy's debate between Cotton Mather and Benjamin Franklin to settle an issue that history had long since decided. The dark Calvinism which drives Ahab to seek the enigmatic whale as the sign of the evil tormenting him is equally remote, set afloat on the *Pequod* to act out its fatal consequences far at sea and away from the troublesome immediacy of nineteenth-century New Bedford. But if theological dogma — and, more broadly, any absolute faith — seemed as cold and remote to Yankee America as the witches buried on Gallows Hill, the desperate search for certainty and assurance that had put the witches there did not. As Philip Gura has shown, in the first half of the nineteenth century American theologians had struggled to reconstruct the imaginative, affective power which had been stripped from religious doctrine and especially from scriptural language by the rationalist empiricism of Unitarian exegetes. That effort was in part an extension of the Coleridgean emphasis on the power of the imagination that had been introduced in America by James Marsh's edition of *Aids to Reflection* in 1829, but it also reflected the more general and justified fear that a historical and philological construal of Scripture such as proposed by Unitarians like Andrews Norton of Harvard threatened to undermine the transcendent ground of religious faith and the social stability which the timeless mystery of that faith made possible. This conflict between literal and symbolic readings of the Bible became a popular controversy as well as the dominant point of contention among theologians, and with a combination of Dutch Reformed and Unitarian relatives in his family, the controversy hit particularly close to home for the young Melville.

By the middle of the century, this debate had exhausted itself within its theological context, but it persisted as a topic of public anxiety to the extent that Gura can attribute the prominence of Hawthorne and Melville as "practitioners of the symbolic mode" to their ability "to translate the widespread concern over the crisis in religious language and doctrine into the realm of imaginative fiction" where it could be explored aesthetically as the crucial human issue it was. *Moby-Dick* and *The Confidence-Man* are obvious examples of Melville's interest in this topic, but "Bartleby the Scrivener" marks an important transitional point in his exploration of the social and metaphysical consequences of living in a world where the connection between signs and significance was no longer secure. In the tragic end of the hubris with which Ahab fused the meaning of evil and the white whale, Melville could recognize the heroic desperation behind the mad futility of belief in any absolute symbolic security. But eight years later, Melville had arrived at the cynical pessimism of *The Confidence-Man*; and faith, either demonic or divine, "had become inexpedient, if not impossible, in a society in which language was reduced to rhetorical chicanery, attached neither to thing nor to spirit but only to the selfish whims of those who exploited it for their own purposes." If, as Cecilia Tichi argues, Melville wrote *The Confidence-Man* to show his readers "what the immoral Wall Street spirit and its ramifications had done to language in America," "Bartleby" uses the inner conflict of the narrator to measure that decay against what had been lost, but not yet forgotten.

As a lawyer who lives his life in a "snug retreat" doing a "snug business among rich men's bonds," Melville's narrator appears to have settled within and indeed lives off of the very medium of the selfishness Gura describes as the norm of the later novel. Yet, after Bartleby enters his life, the narrator's comfort in the smooth-running machinery of that legal discourse gradually gives way to a suspicion that an invisible depth gapes beneath it. Touched by his own sense of a "Puritanic gloom," at one point the narrator turns to Jonathan Edwards for solace and advice and conducts a persistent if somewhat self-conscious and embarrassed quest for Bartleby's soul as a means of restoring discipline to his office and a placid surface to his life. But what worked in Salem fails on Wall Street.

In this story, however, that failure is not the inevitable result of a supernatural faith refusing the inevitable motion of history, nor is it the predestined self-destruction of Ahab's Calvinism fatally entangled in the futility of its own certainty. Instead, the failure of what might be called the Puritan imagination in "Bartleby the Scrivener" works as a subtle condemnation of the legalistic and monetary thought which has supplanted that faith, and in a daring inversion of our usual sympathies, Melville forces us to read the narrator's ceaseless interrogation of Bartleby exactly as the Puritan magistrates defended their own inquisition: as an effort to know in order to save, not just the individual soul in question, but all of humanity.

Though until now no one has noticed the parallel between the narrator's struggle to explain Bartleby and the Puritans' persecution of the witches in Salem, a number of critics have pointed out the desperate tautology of the narrator's questions, which try to constitute their own answers even as they seek them. In his excellent article of 1965, Norman Springer noted that the "narrator's occupation, his immediate concerns and his total profession, can be seen as his attempt to make meaning where there is no meaning," and three years earlier Kingsley Widmer portrayed the specific forms of the narrator's effort as representative of a particular moment in American intellectual history:

> Bartleby reveals the confession of a decent, prudent, rational "liberal" who finds in his chambers of consciousness the incomprehensible, perverse, irrational demon of denial, and of his own denied humanity. . . . He does his best and attempts to exorcise that rebellious and infuriating image with conventional assumptions, authority, utility, legalism, religious orthodoxy, prudent charity, flight, and, at the end, sentimental reverence. . . . The attempt to wryly force benevolent American rationalism to an awareness of our forlorn and walled-in humanity provides the larger purpose of the tale.

I believe these readings are right, up to point. They correctly indicate the coercive nature of the narrator's questions, and they show how the theological concept of the invisible world had been supplanted as a disciplinary mechanism by the various modes of thought Widmer lists. But they do not ask a rather obvious question: why does the narrator fail in his exorcism of this rebel image when everyone else in the story succeeds? After all, the narrator "was not unemployed in his profession by the late John Jacob Astor," and as a lawyer he is proficient in the discourse by which Wall Street operates. Yet everyone knows what to do with Bartleby except him. The second time Bartleby refuses to proofread some legal copy, for example, the narrator is confounded: "*Why* do you refuse?" he asks, and Bartleby replies as usual, "I would prefer not to." "With any other man," the narrator claims, "I should have flown outright into a dreadful passion, scorned all further words, and thrust him ignominiously from my presence. But there was something about Bartleby that not only strangely disarmed me, but, in a wonderful manner, touched and disconcerted me. I began to reason with him" (p. 113). Bartleby, of course, continues to prefer not to, and the narrator calls on his clerks Turkey and Nippers: " 'Nippers' said I, 'what do *you* think of it' 'I think I should kick him out of the office,' " Nippers replies, it being morning and, hence, an ill-tempered time for Nippers because of his indigestion (p. 114).

The narrator calls on Nippers, of course, because he knows exactly how Nippers will respond. The lives of both his regular scriveners are absolutely determined by a mechanistic natural causality, and he has fitted their idiosyncrasies to his office routine. Moreover, he knows that they assume the entire world works the way they do; so they can be counted on to deal with Bartleby with dispatch and dependability. The key to their success, he believes, is their freedom from any consideration larger than the machinery that runs their own lives; so he tries his hand at a similar reduction: worried that he might kill Bartleby out of sheer frustration, he recalls the biblical command to "love one another" and says "yes, this it was that saved me. Aside from higher conderations, charity often operates as a vastly wise and prudent principle — a great safeguard to its possessor. Men have committed murder for jealousy's sake . . . but no man, that I ever heard of, ever committed a diabolical murder for sweet charity's sake. Mere self-interest, then, if no better motive can be enlisted, should . . . prompt all being to charity and philanthropy" (p. 130). Similarly, after struggling between his reluctance to throw Bartleby out of his office and his realization that such an action would solve his problem simply and quickly, he tries to reconcile the conflict by converting his humane concern for Bartleby's welfare into the economic conservatism by which he runs his office and his life:

> [Bartleby's] aspect sufficiently evinces that his eccentricities are involuntary. He is useful to me. I can get along with him. If I turn him away, the chances are he will fall in with some less indulgent employer, and then he will be rudely treated, and perhaps driven forth miserably to starve. Yes. Here I can cheaply purchase a delicious self-approval. To befriend Bartleby; to humor him in his strange willfulness, will cost me little or nothing, while I lay up in my soul what will eventually prove a sweet morsel for my conscience (p. 115).

If the Confidence Man lives in a world where "language is manipulated primarily toward selfish ends and not to express the timeless truths of the natural and moral worlds," then surely here is his compatriot. But unlike the Confidence Man, the lawyer cannot sustain this discourse as a screen against his suspicion that a "higher consideration" is indeed a part of the words. Instead of taking comfort in these rationalizations and laying up some moral capital by rewriting Bartleby's silence into the safety of their syntax, the narrator admits "I felt strangely goaded on to encounter him in new opposition — to elicit some angry spark from him answerable to my own" (p. 115). One afternoon, he says, "the evil impulse" mastered him, and he turns to Turkey to ask him what he thinks of Bartleby's refusal to work. "It was afternoon, be it remembered. Turkey sat glowing like a brass boiler, his bald head steaming, his hands reeling among his blotted papers. 'Think of it?'

roared Turkey, 'I think I'll just step behind the screen, and black his eyes for him!'" Once again, the narrator asks for this advice not because he wonders what Turkey will say but precisely because he does know. The very inevitability of the response is what delights him, and the resolution with which such predetermined courses of action are carried out becomes and object of the narrator's envy. After he gives up his office to get away from Bartleby, for example, his landlord has the scrivener arrested. "The landlord's energetic, summary disposition," the narrator reflects, "had led him to adopt a procedure which I do not think I would have decided upon my self; and yet, as a last resort, under such peculiar circumstances it seemed the only plan" (pp. 136-37).

The narrator's problem is simple. There are a number of ways Bartleby's behavior can be explained, categorized, and easily managed: natural determinism, economic utility, the narrator's "economized" morality, and the law. The narrator, however, cannot make Bartleby fit those categories as easily as other people can because the narrator views Bartleby the same way a Puritan magistrate would — as a sign hiding its true significance — and those explanatory systems cannot accommodate such a sign. Everyone else treats Bartleby as a "mere sign" (as the Puritans would say) which exists simply within the causal chain they happen to apply to it. This contrast emerges vividly when the narrator is considering the possibility of having Bartleby arrested. "No visible means of support; there I have him. Wrong again: for indubitably he *does* support himself, and that is the only unanswerable proof that any man can show of possessing the means so to do" (p. 132). As it turns out, of course, Bartleby does get arrested because, among other reasons, he does not have a visible means of support, and on Wall Street the law does not recognize invisible means, regardless of how they did it in Salem.

The narrator's Puritan turn of mind — and its irrelevance to those around him — is especially evident in his reaction to Bartleby's words. One day, he suddenly realizes that everyone in the office is using the word "prefer":

> Somehow, of late, I had got into the way of involuntarily using this word "prefer" upon all sorts of not exactly suitable occasions. And I trembled to think that my contact with the scrivener had already and seriously affected me in a mental way.... As Nippers, looking very sour and sulky, was departing, Turkey blandly and deferentially approached. "With

submission, sir," said he, "yesterday I was thinking about Bartleby here, and I think that if he would but prefer to take a quart of good ale every day, it would do much towards mending him. . . ."

"So you have got the word, too," said I, slightly excited.

"With submission, and word, sir?" asked Turkey. . . . "What word, sir?"

"I would prefer to be left alone here," said Bartleby, as if offended at being mobbed in his privacy.

"*That's* the word, Turkey," said I — "*that's* it."

"Oh, *prefer?* oh yes — queer word. I never use it myself. But, sir, as I was saying, if he would but prefer — "

"Turkey," interrupted I, "you will please withdraw."

"Oh certainly, sir, if you prefer that I should" (pp. 123-124).

The narrator is not offended at the word itself. As he points out, he is worried that it seems to appear in "not exactly suitable" situations, and it belongs to Bartleby. (In fact, the narrator comes to imagine that *all* language alludes to Bartleby. At one point he is wandering through the streets wondering how he can evict the scrivener when he hears someone say "I'll take odds he doesn't." "Doesn't go? — Done!" the narrator exclaims; "put up your money" [p. 127]. Not until his hand is already in his pocket does he realize the people are talking about an election, not Bartleby.) For the clerks in the office, "prefer" is just another word, literally indistinguishable from others, as Turkey's response makes clear. The relationship between one element in the signifying chain of language and some occasion or source beyond it is irrelevant for the clerks — as might be expected, since they spend most of their time merely copying language with no concern for its origin or meaning, only for the exact correspondence among the copies. The narrator, however, attributes the presence of the word to some dark and mysterious force threatening his mind and the mind of his men: "I thought to myself, surely I must get rid of a demented man, who already has in some degree turned the tongues, if not the heads, of myself and clerks" (p. 124).

Had this unusual possession of the clerks' tongues occurred one hundred fifty years earlier in Salem, the narrator's conclusion would have been enough to get Bartleby arrested as a witch, if not convicted. But unlike the Puritan magistrates, the narrator has no acceptable perspective from which to make that accusation, no way to link "prefer" to Bartleby. As the preceding passage shows, the "event" — the appearance of the word "prefer" — cannot be seen as an event without connecting it to an origin or cause beyond the material domain of speech; yet everyone around the narrator is strictly limited to that domain. As Turkey leaves, having declared that he never uses the word "prefer," the narrator says, "Nippers at his desk caught a glimpse of me, and asked whether I would prefer to have a certain paper copied on blue paper or white. He did not in the least roguishly accent the word prefer. It was plain that it involuntarily rolled from his tongue" (p. 124). From this the narrator concludes that Bartleby must have possessed the minds of his clerks and himself; to Turkey and Nippers, they are merely speaking, borne along by a language that seems to have a mind of its own.

The narrator's suspicion about Bartleby's mysterious power is more than just paranoia. He *must* ascribe invisible causes to the signs of Bartleby's presence if he is to maintain discipline in his own office. The desperate motive behind the narrator's obsession is evident at many places in the story, but it is particularly clear when the narrator confronts Bartleby's disobedience for the first time:

> I looked at Bartleby steadfastly. His face was leanly composed; his gray eyes dimly calm. Not a wrinkle of agitation rippled him. Had there been the least uneasiness, anger, impatience or impertinence in his manner; in other words, had there been anything ordinarily human about him, doubtless I should have violently dismissed him from the premises. But as it was, I should have as soon thought of turning my pale plaster-of-paris bust of Cicero out of doors (p. 112).

Just as the word "prefer" seems to have no distinguishable characteristics at all — it stands out only within the invisible world the narrator tries to find — Bartleby's demeanor lacks any mark which might indicate something beyond it. What confounds the narrator here is that nothing in Bartleby's face signifies some hidden humanity. Like the bust of Cicero, Bartleby is all surface, and that surface is a smooth blank with no deep significance beyond its simple visibility. As the narrator says at the beginning of his story, "what my own astonished eyes saw of Bartleby, *that* is all I know of him" (p. 104).

This remark is not exactly true: Bartleby's appearance is not the only thing the narrator knows about him. One Sunday the narrator is on his way to church when he decides to stop by the office. He finds Bartleby there, makes him leave for a time, and then begins rummaging through the scrivener's few possessions while "presentiments of strange discoveries" hover around him. He finally gets to Bartleby's desk, which is locked, although the key is left in the lock. After making sure that his moral and legal rights are in order ("I mean no mischief . . . besides, the desk is mine"), he opens it. He finds a number of documents and deep pigeonholes. He digs into them, and there, at the deepest interior of Bartleby's most private place, the narrator finds a single object: a saving's bank. This discovery leads him to the conclusion that "the scrivener was the victim of innate and incurable disorder. I might give alms to his body, but his body did not pain him — it was his soul that suffered, and his soul I could not reach" (p. 122).

Having decided that the scrivener's soul is out of reach, the narrator finally gives up trying to help Bartleby and decides to "give him a twenty dollar bill over and above whatever I might owe him" before forcing him to leave. This sudden breach of economic order suggests that his find has hit the narrator where he lives. Whereas before he was confident that his treatment of Bartleby would lay up some ethical capital to be spent on later charges to his conscience, he now recognizes the futility of trying to apply such thinking to the clerk. He cannot give alms for Bartleby's soul because his soul, like the money in his hoard, is out of circulation.

Bartleby's failure to circulate in any sense is a persistent obstacle to the narrator's efforts to get to know him. When he discovers the bank and realizes the futility of his search, the narrator immediately begins to reflect on how little he knows about the scrivener. He attributes that ignorance to Bartleby's silent stillness, and he ascribes the opportunity for this one discovery he has made to one of Bartleby's rare movements:

> I now recalled all the quiet mysteries which I had noted in the man. I remembered that he never spoke but to answer . . . for long periods he would stand looking out . . . upon the dead brick wall; I was quite sure he never visited any refectory or eating house . . . that he never went anywhere in particular that I could learn; never went out for a walk, unless indeed that was the case at present (p. 121).

The narrator, on the other hand, is in constant movement. After offering Bartleby the extra twenty dollars and being turned down, the narrator observes of the scrivener "he made no motion" and tells us that he then left Bartleby in the office, walked out of the door and walked home. After Bartleby's next refusal, the narrator goes out to walk around the block to try to escape from the "wondrous ascendancy" the scrivener has over him. Later, when he returns to the office one last time to persuade Bartleby to come home with him, he gets the usual response: "at present," Bartleby tells him, "I prefer not to make any change at all." This is the last straw, and it sends the narrator into a frenzy of motion:

> I answered nothing; but, effectually dodging every one by the suddenness and rapidity of my flight, rushed from the build-ing, ran up Wall Street towards Broadway, and, jumping in-to the first omnibus, was soon removed from pursuit . . . for a few days, I drove about the upper part of the town and through the suburbs in my rockaway carriage; crossed over to Jersey City and Hoboken, and paid fugitive visits to Manhat-tanville and Astoria. In fact, I almost lived in my rockaway for the time (p. 136).

This time, the narrator makes good his escape. When he returns, Bartleby has been arrested. The narrator's conversion of his life into frantic motion has been matched by the smooth-turning wheels of the legal machine. In Melville's story this is as it must be. The world of business runs on the law of motion: for the "exchange banking and business commission," knowledge meant money; money meant ex-change; and exchange meant the quick shuffle of empty signs. On Wall Street stillness and a silent soul were capital crimes.

Given the narrator's pride in his professional status, it is remarkable that he only brings up two trials in the course of his story. The first one he recalls when confronting Bartleby alone in the office one day and worrying that his scrivener may get violent. It is the famous trial of John C. Colt, who murdered a printer named Samuel Adams, stuffed his body in a crate, and planned to mail it — a real dead letter — to New Orleans. The other trial is mentioned by the grub-man when the narrator in-troduces him to Bartleby for the first time. It involves the case of the famous forger Monroe Edwards, whom Horace Greeley called "the most distinguished financier since the days of Judas Iscariot." After being told that Bartleby prefers not to dine today, the grub-man says, " 'How's this . . . He's odd, ain't he?' 'I think he is a little deranged,' said I, sadly. 'Deranged? deranged is it? Well, now, upon my word, I thought that friend of yourn was a gentelman forger; they are always pale and genteel-like, them forgers. . . . Did you know Monroe Edwards?' " (pp. 138-39).

The difference between these two trials is significant: the narrator associates Bartleby with a crime against humanity, and the grub-man associates the scrivener with a crime against — and literally *on* paper. This has been the narrator's problem all along. The humanity that he would impute to Bartleby simply is out of place in the business world around him. Within that world, and within the various systems of law and language that make it run, Bartleby is truly "deranged," that is, out of order, as long as one looks at him to see beyond the surface. Others look at him very differently, and that is why he passes into their comprehension so easily. The grub-man's perception of Bartleby as a forger is a telling example of this more "useful" perspective. For Bartleby fits into the world of Wall Street as — and only as — a forgery. Everyone "signs" him (i.e., makes him significant) in their own terms; he is a link in various deterministic chains, a slackard, a trespasser, or, mistaking the mark for the man, a forger. Once signed in like this, Bartleby presents no problem because no one except the narrator cares where words come from, only how they work. This is, of course, the mark of a successful forgery. If a forger's signature ever points its reader beyond the document to the person who signed it, the forger is in trouble. His "sign" must point only to the other signs in the contracts on which it lives. For the narrator, Bartleby's blank pallor is a window to a world beyond Wall Street; for everyone else in the story, the blank that is Bartleby is only the white space at the bottom of a page signed by a passing hand that has gone about its business.

Melville's Wall Street is a world where names, as the narrator tells us, "ring like gold bullion" (p. 104) rather than sound the depth of their owner's soul, and humanity has no more value than an ephemeral reflection shimmering on the surface of a newly polished coin. Yet the narrator is drawn by that trembling image to study Bartleby for some sign of the revelation that Cotton Mather promised us in the scriptural letter that begins his sermon in *Wonders of the Invisible World*. After citing his text (Rev. 12:12) Mather claims,

> We have in our Hands a Letter from our Ascended Lord in Heaven, to advise us of his being still alive, and of his Purpose e're long, to give us a Visit, wherein we shall see our Living Redeemer, stand at the latter day upon the Earth. . . . And altho' it have, as 'tis expressed by one of the Ancients, Tot Sacramenta quot verba, a Mystery in every Syllable, yet it is not altogether to be neglected with such a Despair, as that, I cannot Read, for the Book is Sealed. It is a Revelation, and a singular, and notable Blessing is pronounc'd upon them that humbly study it.

This was the same advice that Horace Bushnell and other Christian transcendentalists posed against their more literal-minded contemporaries, and Melville's narrator does his best to follow it, straining to hear that revelation in the implacable stillness of Bartleby's silence. As we saw in the trial of Susannah Martin, silence was by no means illegible for the Puritan magistrates. Martin's refusal to tell them her thoughts was the very opening in which their interpretation of her testimony came together with the thoughts of the congregation to combine knowledge and power in the magistrates' judgment and to restore stability to the community. But in "Bartleby the Scrivener," such interpretive strategies and transcendent meanings are alien to the orders of power by which society operates; the efficient hum of busy capitalism in nineteenth-century America needed no silent partner.

Melville's nostalgia for a community of interpretation that could live the connection between world and Word at a depth that would meet humanity's spiritual needs required no specifically Puritan source. He had grown up listening to theologians whose theories of exegesis yielded utopian projects of social harmony and lay orators who traced the problems of society to a clumsy grasp of scriptural terms. But the hermeneutic integration of spiritual insight and social power that Mather describes at the heart of the witchcraft trials was a unique moment in which those theories had been fact, and the Puritan experiment lies behind Melville's story like the witches buried beneath the hill on which Hawthorne's narrator tells the story of Alice Doane. If Melville could gibe Hawthorne for his Puritanic gloom, he could also recognize in that darkness the memory of a time that had eclipsed the glittering trivialities of everyday life in the light of revelation and glory.

There is, of course, a revelation of sorts at the end of "Bartleby": the narrator tells us about the rumor that Bartleby has worked at the Dead Letter Office in Washington. But in Melville's tale, there is no living Word behind the letters. Bartleby is as lifeless as the mail he processed, and like those letters he is cut off from his origins and diverted from his end. There is, to be sure, a great conflagration in this revelation; the narrator tells us that the letters Bartleby sorts are burned by the cartload. For the Puritans, though, the conflagration at the end of time had been the light by which we see the truth of our moment. For the postal system, the fire that burns the wayward letters is simply a means of casting out the evidence of the system's limitations and so occluding any critical perspective on its workings. It consumes everything that threatens to escape the subordinate hand feeding its flames. Unlike

Mather's letter, these remain sealed, sealed just as tightly as the narrator's chambers, which look upon a blank white air shaft at one end and confront a wall of soot-blackened bricks at the other. As the view from these windows proves, there is no outside on Wall Street. And with such a view, there can be no vision.

Chronology

1819	Herman Melville (or Melvill) born on August 1 in New York City, the third child of Allan Melville, an importer, and Maria Gansevoort Melville.
1826	Melville attends the New York Male High School.
1830–32	Allan Melville's importing business fails, and he moves the family to Albany. Herman becomes a student at the Albany Academy until his father's death in 1832. Then he works at various jobs: a bank clerk, a helper on his brother's farm, and an assistant in his brother's fur factory and store.
1835–38	Continues his education at various high schools; supplements the family income by teaching.
1839	"Fragments from a Writing Desk" published May 4 and May 18 in the *Democratic Press and Lansingburgh Advertiser*. Melville works his way to Liverpool and back on the *Saint Lawrence*, a merchant ship.
1841–44	Melville leaves Fairhaven, Massachusetts, as a sailor on the whaler *Acushnet*, bound for the South Seas. Jumps ship in the Marquesas Islands, where he lives among the natives for about a month. After a series of adventures, travels home as a passenger on the frigate *United States*.
1846	Publishes *Typee*. Brother Gansevoort dies.
1847	Publishes *Omoo*. Marries Elizabeth Shaw, daughter of Chief Justice Lemuel Shaw of Boston.
1847–50	Melville tries to earn a living as a writer, producing occasional articles and reviews. Makes acquaintance of George and Evert Duyckinck, and other New York literary figures.
1849	Publishes *Mardi* and *Redburn*. Travels to Europe. Son Malcolm born.

1850	Publishes *White-Jacket*. Purchases Arrowhead, a farm near Pittsfield, Massachusetts. Begins his friendship with Nathaniel Hawthorne, who lives in nearby Lenox.
1851	Publishes *Moby-Dick*. Son Stanwix born.
1852	Publishes *Pierre*.
1853–56	Daughter Elizabeth born. Writes stories and sketches for *Putnam's Monthly Magazine* and *Harper's New Monthly Magazine*.
1855	Publishes *Israel Potter* as a book, after serialization in *Putnam's*. Daughter Frances born.
1856	*The Piazza Tales* published. Melville travels to Europe and the Near East for his health.
1857	*The Confidence-Man*, which Melville left with his publisher before he began travelling, is finally published. Melville returns to the United States.
1857–60	Melville supports family by lectures on such topics as "Statuary in Rome," "The South Seas," and "Travelling."
1863	Melville sells Arrowhead and moves his family to New York City.
1866	Publishes a collection of poems, *Battle-Pieces and Aspects of the War*. Son Malcolm shoots himself; Stanwix runs away to sea.
1876	Publishes *Clarel*.
1886	Stanwix dies.
1888	*John Marr and Other Sailors* privately printed.
1891	*Timoleon* privately printed. Melville dies on September 28.
1924	First publication of *Billy Budd*.

Contributors

HAROLD BLOOM, Sterling Professor of the Humanities at Yale University, is the author of *The Anxiety of Influence, Poetry and Repression,* and many other volumes of literary criticism. His forthcoming study, *Freud: Transference and Authority*, attempts a full-scale reading of all of Freud's major writings. A MacArthur Prize Fellow, he is general editor of five series of literary criticism published by Chelsea House.

JORGE LUIS BORGES, who died in 1986, was one of the most important writers of this century. The author of poetry, fictions, and essays, his best known work in English is *Labyrinths*.

LEO MARX is William R. Kenan, Jr., Professor of American Cultural History at MIT. He is the author of *The Machine in the Garden: Technology and the Pastoral Ideal in America*.

WARNER BERTHOFF is Professor of English at Harvard University. He is the author of *The Ferment of Realism: American Literature, 1884–1919* and *A Literature without Qualities: American Writing since 1945*.

BARBARA JOHNSON is Professor of Romance Languages and Literature at Harvard University. She is the author of *The Critical Difference* and *Défigurations de Langage Poétique: La Seconde Révolution Baudelairienne*.

ERIC J. SUNDQUIST teaches English at the University of California at Berkeley. He is the author of *Home as Found: Authority and Genealogy in Nineteenth-Century American Literature* and *Faulkner: The House Divided*.

MICHAEL PAUL ROGIN is Professor of Political Science at the University of California at Berkeley. In addition to *Subversive Genealogies*, he is the author of *The Intellectual and McCarthy: The Radical Specter* and *Fathers and Children: Andrew Jackson and the Destruction of the American Indian*.

MICHAEL CLARK is Professor of English at Widener College.

Bibliography

Arvin, Newton. *Herman Melville*. New York: William Sloane, 1950.

Auden, W. H. *The Enchafed Flood, or The Romantic Iconography of the Sea*. New York: Vintage, 1967.

Bickley, R. Bruce, Jr. *The Method of Melville's Short Fiction, 1853–1856*. Durham, N.C.: Duke University Press, 1975.

Blackmur, R. P. "The Craft of Herman Melville: A Putative Statement." In *The Lion and the Honeycomb: Essays in Solicitude and Critique*, 124–44. New York: Harcourt, Brace & World, 1955.

Bowen, Merlin. *The Long Encounter: Self and Experience in the Writings of Herman Melville*. Chicago: University of Chicago Press, 1960.

Branch, Watson G., ed. *Melville: The Critical Heritage*. London and Boston: Routledge & Kegan Paul, 1974.

Braswell, William. *Melville's Religious Thought: An Essay in Interpretation*. Durham, N.C.: Duke University Press, 1943.

Brodhead, Richard H. *Hawthorne, Melville, and the Novel*. Chicago: University of Chicago Press, 1976.

Brooks, Van Wyck. *The Times of Melville and Whitman*. New York: Dutton, 1947.

Chase, Richard. *Herman Melville: A Critical Study*. New York: Macmillan, 1949.

———, ed. *Melville: A Collection of Critical Essays*. Englewood Cliffs, N.J.: Prentice-Hall, 1962.

Clark, Michael. "Authorial Displacement in Herman Melville's 'The Piazza.'" *CLA Journal* 27 (1983): 69–80.

Coxe, Louis O., and Robert Chapman. *Billy Budd: A Play in Three Acts*. Princeton: Princeton University Press, 1951.

DeKoven, Marianne. "History as Suppressed Referent in Modernist Fiction." *ELH* 51, no. 1 (1984): 137–52.

Dillingham, William B. *Melville's Short Fiction, 1853–1856*. Athens: University of Georgia Press, 1977.

Donaldson, Scott. "The Dark Truth of *The Piazza Tales*." *PMLA* 85 (1970): 1082–86.

Douglas, Ann. "Herman Melville and the Revolt against the Reader." In *The Feminization of American Culture*, 289–326. New York: Knopf, 1978.

Dryden, Edgar A. *Melville's Thematics of Form: The Great Art of Telling the Truth*. Baltimore: Johns Hopkins University Press, 1968.

Emery, Allan Moore. "'Benito Cereno' and Manifest Destiny." *Nineteenth-Century Fiction* 39 (1984): 48–68.

153

Feidelson, Charles, Jr. *Symbolism and American Literature*. Chicago: University of Chicago Press, 1953.

Fiedler, Leslie A. "Blackness of Darkness: The Negro and the Development of American Gothic." In *Images of the Negro in American Literature*, edited by Seymour L. Gross and John Edward Hardy, 84–105. Chicago: University of Chicago Press, 1966.

Finkelstein, Dorothee Metlitsky. *Melville's Orienda*. New Haven: Yale University Press, 1961.

Fisher, Marvin. *Going Under: Melville's Short Fiction and the American 1850s*. Baton Rouge: Louisiana State University Press, 1977.

Fogle, Richard Harter. "*Billy Budd*: The Order of the Fall." *Nineteenth-Century Fiction* 15 (1960): 189–205.

———. *Melville's Shorter Tales*. Norman: University of Oklahoma Press, 1960.

Forster, E. M. *Aspects of the Novel*. New York: Harcourt, Brace & World, 1927.

Forster, E. M., and Eric Crozier. Libretto for *Billy Budd: Opera in Four Acts*, music by Benjamin Britten. London: Boosey & Hawkes, 1951.

Franklin, H. Bruce. *The Wake of the Gods: Melville's Mythology*. Stanford, Calif.: Stanford University Press, 1963.

Fussell, Mary Everett Burton. "*Billy Budd*: Melville's Happy Ending." *Studies in Romanticism* 15 (1976): 43–57.

Galloway, David D. "Herman Melville's 'Benito Cereno': An Anatomy." *Texas Studies in Literature and Language* 9 (1967): 239–52.

Glick, Wendell. "Expediency and Absolute Morality in *Billy Budd*." *PMLA* 68 (1953): 103–10.

Hardwick, Elizabeth. "Bartleby and Manhattan." In *Bartleby and Manhattan and Other Essays*, 217–31. New York: Random House, 1983.

Hayford, Harrison, ed. *The Somers Mutiny Affair*. Englewood Cliffs, N.J.: Prentice-Hall, 1959.

Hetherington, Hugh W. *Melville's Reviewers, British and American, 1846–1891*. Chapel Hill: University of North Carolina Press, 1961.

Hoffman, Daniel G. *Form and Fable in American Fiction*. New York: Oxford University Press, 1961.

Howard, Leon. *Herman Melville: A Biography*. Berkeley: University of California Press, 1951.

Hyman, Stanley Edgar. "Melville the Scrivener." In *The Promised End: Essays and Reviews, 1942–1962*, 68–99. Freeport, N.Y.: Books for Libraries Press, 1972.

Inge, M. Thomas, ed. *Bartleby the Inscrutable: A Collection of Commentary on Herman Melville's Tale "Bartleby the Scrivener."* Hamden, Conn.: Shoe String Press, Archon, 1979.

Karcher, Carolyn L. *Shadow over the Promised Land: Slavery, Race, and Violence in Melville's America*. Baton Rouge: Louisiana State University Press, 1980.

Kazin, Alfred. "'Melville Is Dwelling Somewhere in New York.'" In *An American Procession*, 131–60. New York: Knopf, 1984.

Lawrence, D. H. *Studies in Classic American Literature*. New York: Thomas Seltzer, 1923.

Lee, A. Robert, ed. *Herman Melville: Reassessments*. London and Totowa, N.J.: Vision and Barnes & Noble, 1984.

Levin, Harry. *The Power of Blackness: Hawthorne, Poe, and Melville*. New York: Knopf, 1958.

Lewis, R. W. B. *The American Adam: Innocence, Tragedy, and Tradition in the Nineteenth*

Century. Chicago: University of Chicago Press, 1955.

———. *Trials of the Word: Essays in American Literature and the Humanistic Tradition*. New Haven: Yale University Press, 1965.

Leyda, Jay. *The Melville Log: A Documentary Life of Herman Melville, 1819–1891*. 2 vols. New York: Harcourt, Brace, 1951.

Limon, John. "The American Stutter." *Genre* 18 (1985): 215–33.

Matthiessen, F. O. *American Renaissance: Art and Expression in the Age of Emerson and Whitman*. New York: Oxford University Press, 1941.

McWilliams, John P., Jr. *Hawthorne, Melville, and the American Character: A Looking-Glass Business*. Cambridge: Cambridge University Press, 1984.

Melville, Herman. *Billy Budd, Sailor (An Inside Narrative)*. Edited from the manuscript with introduction and notes by Harrison Hayford and Merton M. Sealts, Jr. Chicago: University of Chicago Press, 1962.

———. *Journal of a Visit to London and the Continent, 1849–1850*. Edited by Eleanor Melville Metcalf. Cambridge: Harvard University Press, 1948.

———. *The Letters of Herman Melville*. Edited by Merrel R. David and William H. Gilman. New Haven: Yale University Press, 1960.

Miller, Perry. "Melville and Transcendentalism." In *Nature's Nation*, 184–96. Cambridge: Harvard University Press, 1967.

———. *The Raven and the Whale: The War of Words and Wits in the Era of Poe and Melville*. New York: Harcourt, Brace, 1956.

Montale, Eugenio. "An Introduction to *Billy Budd*." *The Sewanee Review* 68 (1960): 419–22.

Mumford, Lewis. *Herman Melville*. New York: Harcourt, Brace, 1929.

Nnolim, Charles E. *Melville's "Benito Cereno": A Study in the Meaning of Name Symbolism*. New York: New Voices, 1974.

Parker, Hershel. "Melville's Salesman Story." *Studies in Short Fiction* 1 (1964): 154–58.

———, ed. *The Recognition of Herman Melville: Selected Criticism since 1846*. Ann Arbor: University of Michigan Press, 1967.

Pavese, Cesare. "Herman Melville." In *American Literature: Essays and Opinions*, translated by Edwin Fussell. Berkeley: University of California Press, 1970.

Pearson, Norman Holmes. "*Billy Budd*: 'The King's Yarn.'" *American Quarterly* 3 (1951): 99–114.

Pullin, Faith, ed. *New Perspectives on Melville*. Kent, Ohio: Kent State University Press, 1978.

Rosenberry, Edward H. "The Problem of *Billy Budd*." *PMLA* 80 (1965): 489–98.

Rowland, Beryl. "Melville and the Cock that Crew." *American Literature* 52 (1981): 593–606.

Schehr, Lawrence R. "Dead Letters: Theories of Writing in 'Bartleby the Scrivener.'" *Enclitic* 7, no. 1 (1983): 96–103.

Sedgwick, William Ellery. *Herman Melville: The Tragedy of Mind*. Cambridge: Harvard University Press, 1944.

Senn, Werner. "Reading Melville's Mazes: An Aspect of the Short Stories." *English Studies* 65 (1984): 27–35.

Stafford, William T., ed. *Melville's Billy Budd and the Critics*. 2d ed. Belmont, Calif.: Wadsworth, 1969.

Stern, Milton R. *The Fine Hammered Steel of Herman Melville*. Urbana: University of

Illinois Press, 1957.

Thomas, Brook. "The Legal Fictions of Herman Melville and Lemuel Shaw." *Critical Inquiry* 11 (1984): 24–51.

Vanderbilt, Kermit. "'Benito Cereno': Melville's Fable of Black Complicity." *The Southern Review* 12 (1976): 311–22.

Vincent, Howard P., ed. *"Bartleby the Scrivener."* Melville Annual, 1965: A Symposium. Kent, Ohio: Kent State University Press, 1966.

———. *Twentieth-Century Interpretations of* Billy Budd. Englewood Cliffs, N.J.: Prentice-Hall, 1971.

Welsh, Howard. "The Politics of Race in 'Benito Cereno.'" *American Literature* 46 (1975): 556–66.

Widmer, Kingsley. *The Ways of Nihilism: A Study of Herman Melville's Short Novels.* Los Angeles: California State Colleges, 1970.

Winters, Yvor. "Herman Melville and the Problem of Moral Navigation." In *In Defense of Reason*, 200–233. New York: Swallow Press and William Morrow, 1947.

Withim, Paul. *"Billy Budd*: Testament of Resistance." *Modern Language Quarterly* 20 (1959): 115–27.

Ziff, Larzer. *Literary Democracy: The Declaration of Cultural Independence in America.* New York: Viking, 1981.

Acknowledgments

"Prologue to Herman Melville's 'Bartleby'" by Jorge Luis Borges from *Review: Latin American Literature and Art* 17 (Spring 1976), © 1976 by the Center for Inter-American Relations, Inc. Reprinted by permission. This essay was originally published in Spanish as the prologue to Borges' own translation of Melville's "Bartleby" (Buenos Aires: Emece Editores, 1974).

"Melville's Parable of the Walls" by Leo Marx from *The Sewanee Review* 61, no. 4 (Autumn 1953) © 1953, renewed 1981 by the University of the South. Reprinted by permission of the editor of *The Sewanee Review*.

"'Certain Phenomenal Men': The Example of *Billy Budd*" by Warner Berthoff from *The Example of Melville* by Warner Berthoff, © 1962 by Princeton University Press. Reprinted by permission of Princeton University Press.

"Melville's Fist: The Execution of *Billy Budd*" by Barbara Johnson from *Studies in Romanticism* 18, no. 4 (Winter 1979), © 1979 by the Trustees of Boston University. Reprinted by permission.

"Suspense and Tautology in 'Benito Cereno'" by Eric J. Sundquist from *Glyph: Johns Hopkins Textual Studies,* no. 8 (1981), © 1981 by The Johns Hopkins University Press, Baltimore/London. Reprinted by permission.

"Melville and the Slavery of the North" (originally entitled "Class Struggles in America") by Michael Paul Rogin from *Subversive Genealogy: The Politics and Art of Herman Melville* by Michael Paul Rogin, © 1979, 1980, 1983 by Michael Paul Rogin. Reprinted by permission of Alfred A. Knopf, Inc.

"Witches and Wall Street: Possession Is Nine-Tenths of the Law" by Michael Clark from *Texas Studies in Literature and Language* 25, no. 1 (Spring 1983), © 1983 by the University of Texas Press. Reprinted by permission of the author and the University of Texas Press.

157

Index

Abbot, Benjamin, 132, 133
Adams, John, 110
Adams, Samuel, 144
Aids to Reflection (Coleridge), 136
"Alice Doane's Appeal" (Hawthorne),
    134–35, 146
Amerika (Kafka), 8
Aristotle, 39, 49

"Bartleby the Scrivener," 7–29,
    127–47; abstractness of, 110; ap-
    prentice vs. master in, 110–12,
    123; authority in, 115–16;
    "Bartleby movement" of, 19;
    Bartleby's role in, 8, 14, 16–22,
    23–26, 27, 29, 100, 101–2,
    110–12, 142–47; "Benito Cereno"
    compared with, 100, 101–2, 105;
    charity as theme in, 20, 21, 29,
    114, 139; choice as theme in, 16,
    18, 24–25; Christianity in, 20,
    114; colors in, 13, 14, 27, 28;
    Dead Letter Office as metaphor
    in, 22, 117, 146–47; death as
    theme in, 17–18, 19; democratic
    values in, 112, 114; "doctrine of
    assumptions" in, 19; as early
    work, 12; fate as theme in, 20, 26,
    28; folding screen in, 14–15, 21,
    29, 115; forgery as theme in 111,
    144–45; genre defined by, 8;
    green as symbol in, 14–15, 21, 27,
    28, 29; humanity as theme in, 17,
    29, 144–45; human relationships
    in, 109–10, 114, 116; insanity as
    theme in, 22, 143, 144; "I prefer
    not to" phrase in, 16, 18, 24–25,
    111, 138, 140–42; irony in, 20,
    22; Jacksonian politics in, 109,
    116; Job mentioned in, 117; lack
    of realism in, 110, 114–15;
    language of, 8, 117, 141; lawyer
    as narrator of, 13, 14, 15, 16–22,
    24, 25, 28–29, 100, 101–2,
    110–11, 113–16, 117, 137–46;
    "lawyer's movement" of, 20;
    "Master in Chancery" as title in,
    110, 112–13; metaphor in, 19,
    21–23, 26–27, 28, 107, 111,
    116–17, 146–47; metaphysical
    problems in, 18–19, 23; *Moby-Dick*
    compared with, 14, 15, 23, 25–26,
    28, 29; modernist fiction com-
    pared with, 109–10; narrative of,
    13, 16–22; negativity in, 112;
    nihilism in, 8; Nipper's role in,
    23, 24, 138, 142; objective reality
    in, 15, 29, 110; office floor plan as
    key to, 13–15; as parable of
    Melville's writing career, 11–12,
    18–19, 24, 25; passive resistance
    in, 111–12, 114; personal history
    in, 109–10, 114–15, 117; *Pierre*
    compared with, 107–8, 109, 115;
    political context of, 109, 110, 114,
    116; prison as metaphor in, 19,
    21–23, 26–27, 28, 107, 111,